I0889965

Contents

Introduction 2
The National Geography Standards 4
Week 1 What Is a Map? 6
Week 2 Using a Map 10
Week 3 Finding Places on a Map 14
Week 4 Directions on a Map 18
Week 5 Using Directions 22
Week 6 A Map Key 26
Week 7 Using a Map Key 30
Week 8 Parts of a Map 34
Week 9 Picturing a Place 38
Week 10 Picturing the United States 42
Week 11 A Treasure Map 46
Week 12 A Street Map 50
Week 13 What Is a Globe? 54
Week 14 A World Map 58
Week 15 A Land and Water Map of Colorado . . 62
Week 16 A Land and Water Map of Arizona . . . 66
Week 17 A Land and Water Map of Hawaii 70
Week 18 A Land and Water Map of Oregon 74
Week 19 A Farm Map 78
Week 20 A Town Map 82
Week 21 A City Map 86
Week 22 A State Map 90
Week 23 A Zoo Map 94
Week 24 A Fun Park Map 98
Week 25 A Weather Map 102
Week 26 A Desert Habitat 106
Week 27 Moving to the City 110
Week 28 A County Fair Map 114
Week 29 A Supermarket Map 118
Week 30 Houses in a Community 122
Week 31 Community Helpers 126
Week 32 Farms in Iowa 130
Week 33 Visit California! 134
Week 34 Natural Resources of Alaska 138
Week 35 A Frontier Town 142
Week 36 A Neighborhood Plan 146
Glossary 150

CREDITS
Writing: Sandi Johnson
Editor: Chryl Light
Copy Editing: Sonny Bennett, Cathy Harber
Illustrators: Jim Palmer, Mary Rojas
Designers: Alex Cruz, Cheryl Puckett
Desktop: Kristen Calcatera
Cover: Cheryl Puckett

Evan-Moor®
An imprint of IXL Learning
PO BOX 35665
Greensboro, NC 27425 USA

ISBN 978-1-55799-970-2
01-201267784

About *Daily Geography Practice*

Daily Geography Practice is based on the eighteen National Geography Standards and is designed to support any geography and social studies curriculums that you may be using in your classroom.

36 Weekly Sections

Teacher Page

- An answer key for the week is included for easy reference.

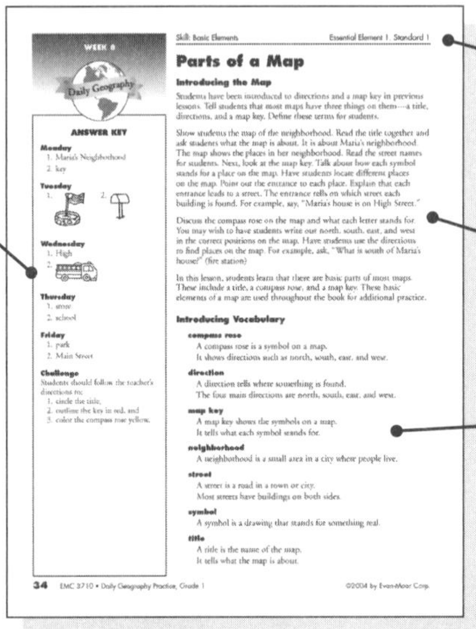

- The national geography element, standard, and skill are included.
- Background information helps the teacher introduce the geography skill.
- Vocabulary words and definitions are given.

Please note that the skills in this book should be taught in direct instruction, and not used as independent practice. Teachers are encouraged to use other reference maps and globes to aid in instruction. Most of the questions can be answered by studying the map or globe. There are some questions, however, that specifically relate to the lesson given by the teacher at the beginning of the week. Review daily the information presented in "Introducing the Map."

Map Page

A map illustrates the geography skills emphasized during the week. Use the map to aid in whole-class instruction, or reproduce a copy for each student to use as a reference for the questions.

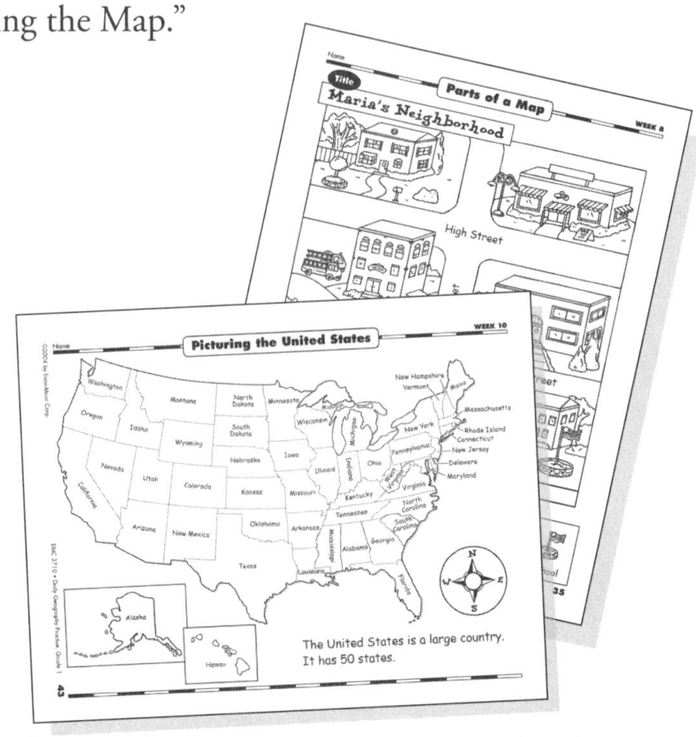

Question Pages

There are two geography questions for each day of the week. The questions progress in difficulty from Monday to Friday. The challenge question at the end of the week asks students to add a feature to the map. Outside references are often required to answer the challenge question.

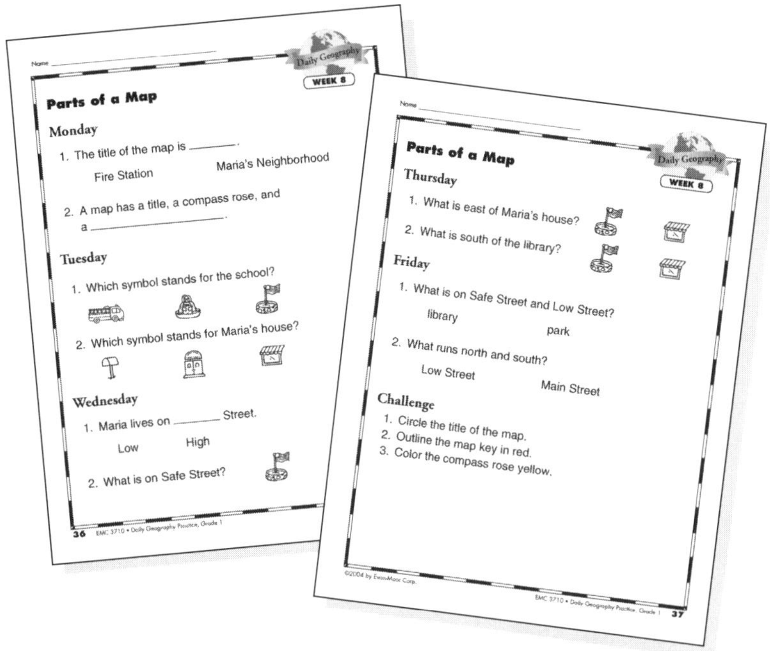

Name ____

Daily Geography

WEEK 8

Parts of a Map

Monday

1. The title of the map is ____.
   Fire Station   Maria's Neighborhood
2. A map has a title, a compass rose, and a ____.

Tuesday

1. Which symbol stands for the school?
2. Which symbol stands for Maria's house?

Wednesday

1. Maria lives on ____ Street.
   Low   High
2. What is on Safe Street?

36 EMC 3710 • Daily Geography Practice, Grade 1

Name ____

Daily Geography

WEEK 8

Parts of a Map

Thursday

1. What is east of Maria's house?
2. What is south of the library?

Friday

1. What is on Safe Street and Low Street?
   library   park
2. What runs north and south?
   Low Street   Main Street

Challenge

1. Circle the title of the map.
2. Outline the map key in red.
3. Color the compass rose yellow.

©2004 by Evan-Moor Corp.

EMC 3710 • Daily Geography Practice, Grade 1 37

Geography Glossary

Reproduce the glossary pages and cover for students to use as an easy reference booklet throughout the year.

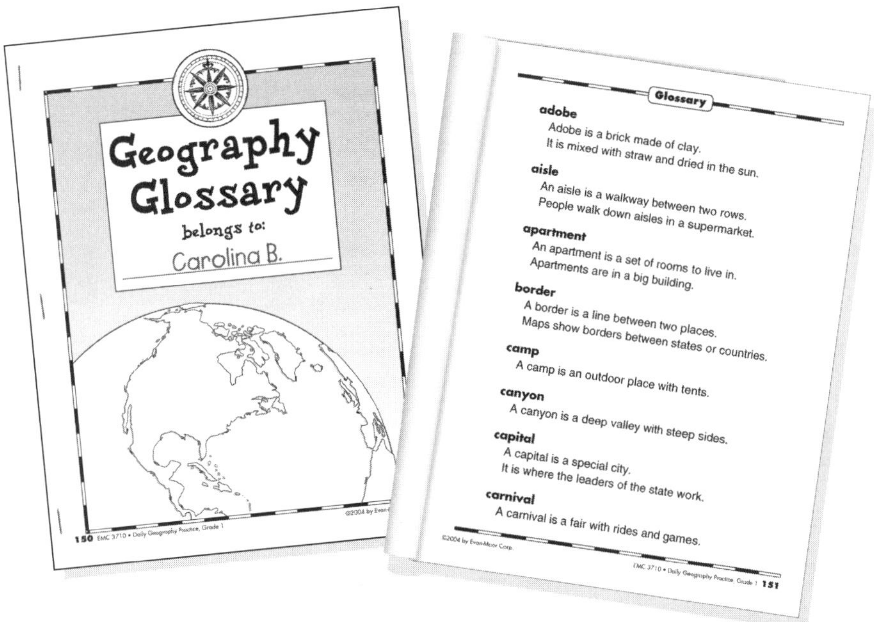

Geography Glossary

belongs to:

Carolina B.

150 EMC 3710 • Daily Geography Practice, Grade 1

Glossary

adobe
Adobe is a brick made of clay.
It is mixed with straw and dried in the sun.

aisle
An aisle is a walkway between two rows.
People walk down aisles in a supermarket.

apartment
An apartment is a set of rooms to live in.
Apartments are in a big building.

border
A border is a line between two places.
Maps show borders between states or countries.

camp
A camp is an outdoor place with tents.

canyon
A canyon is a deep valley with steep sides.

capital
A capital is a special city.
It is where the leaders of the state work.

carnival
A carnival is a fair with rides and games.

©2004 by Evan-Moor Corp.

EMC 3710 • Daily Geography Practice, Grade 1 151

The National Geography Standards

The National Geography Standards includes six essential elements that highlight the major components of geography. Under the six major categories are the eighteen standards that focus on general areas in geography that children are expected to know and understand.

Essential Element 1: The World in Spatial Terms

Geography studies the relationships between people, places, and environments by mapping information about them into a spatial context. The geographically informed person knows and understands the following:

Standard 1 .... **Weeks 1–8**
how to use maps and other geographic representations, tools, and technologies to acquire, process, and report information from a spatial perspective,

Standard 2 .... **Weeks 9–10**
how to use mental maps to organize information about people, places, and environments in a spatial context, and

Standard 3 .... **Weeks 11–12**
how to analyze the spatial organization of people, places, and environments on Earth's surface.

Essential Element 2: Places and Regions

The identities and lives of individuals and peoples are rooted in particular places and in those human constructs called regions. The geographically informed person knows and understands the following:

Standard 4 .... **Weeks 13–18**
the physical and human characteristics of places,

Standard 5 .... **Weeks 19–22**
that people create regions to interpret Earth's complexity, and

Standard 6 .... **Weeks 23–24**
how culture and experience influence people's perceptions of places and regions.

Essential Element 3: Physical Systems

Physical processes shape Earth's surface and interact with plant and animal life to create, sustain, and modify the ecosystems. The geographically informed person knows and understands the following:

Standard 7 .... **Week 25**
the physical processes that shape the patterns of Earth's surface, and

Standard 8 .... **Week 26**
the characteristics and spatial distribution of ecosystems on Earth's surface.

Essential Element 4: Human Systems

People are central to geography in that human activities help shape Earth's surface, human settlements and structures are part of Earth's surface, and humans compete for control of Earth's surface. The geographically informed person knows and understands the following:

Standard 9 . . . . **Week 27**
the characteristics, distribution, and migration of human populations on Earth's surface,

Standard 10 . . . . **Week 28**
the characteristics, distribution, and complexity of Earth's cultural mosaics,

Standard 11 . . . . **Week 29**
the patterns and networks of economic interdependence on Earth's surface,

Standard 12 . . . . **Week 30**
the processes, patterns, and functions of human settlement, and

Standard 13 . . . . **Week 31**
how the forces of cooperation and conflict among people influence the division and control of Earth's surface.

Essential Element 5: Environment and Society

The physical environment is modified by human activities, largely as a consequence of the ways in which human societies value and use Earth's natural resources. Human activities are also influenced by Earth's physical features and processes. The geographically informed person knows and understands the following:

Standard 14 . . . . **Week 32**
how human actions modify the physical environment,

Standard 15 . . . . **Week 33**
how physical systems affect human systems, and

Standard 16 . . . . **Week 34**
the changes that occur in the meaning, use, distribution, and importance of resources.

Essential Element 6: The Uses of Geography

Knowledge of geography enables people to develop an understanding of the relationships between people, places, and environments over time—that is, of Earth as it was, is, and might be. The geographically informed person knows and understands the following:

Standard 17 . . . . **Week 35**
how to apply geography to interpret the past, and

Standard 18 . . . . **Week 36**
how to apply geography to interpret the present and plan for the future.

WEEK 1

Daily Geography

ANSWER KEY

Monday

1. map
2. bedroom

Tuesday

1. 
2. 

Wednesday

1. bed
2. window

Thursday

1. 
2. 

Friday

1. bed
2. table

Challenge

Answers will vary, but students should color a favorite place on the map.

What Is a Map?

Introducing the Map

Ask students to think about their bedrooms at home. What do they look like? What kinds of things are in their bedrooms? They may say things such as a bed, dresser, toys, and a desk. Ask students to think about how they would draw a picture of their bedrooms with everything in it. Tell them it would be easier to think about where things are if they were high above it. Then they could look down and see everything in its place.

Share with students that when they make a special picture like this, it is called a map. A map is a drawing that shows where things are. A map looks like someone drew it from high above.

Show students the map of a bedroom. Read the title and caption. Tell students to pretend they are high above this bedroom. They are looking down on it. Talk about the things that are in the bedroom and where they are found. Read the labels for students.

The questions for this map include the use of positional words. Positional words help describe the location or position of things on a map. The following words and phrases are used: *behind, in front of, next to,* and *on.* Ask students to find the dresser. Then ask them to look for something that is on top of the dresser. Ask other questions using each positional word or phrase.

Students should begin to understand the idea that a map shows how a place looks from above. They will also begin to develop a sense of direction.

Introducing Vocabulary

map

A map is a drawing of a place from above.
A map shows where things are.

Name

What Is a Map?

A map is a drawing of a place from above.

A map shows where things are.

This is a map of Joey's bedroom.

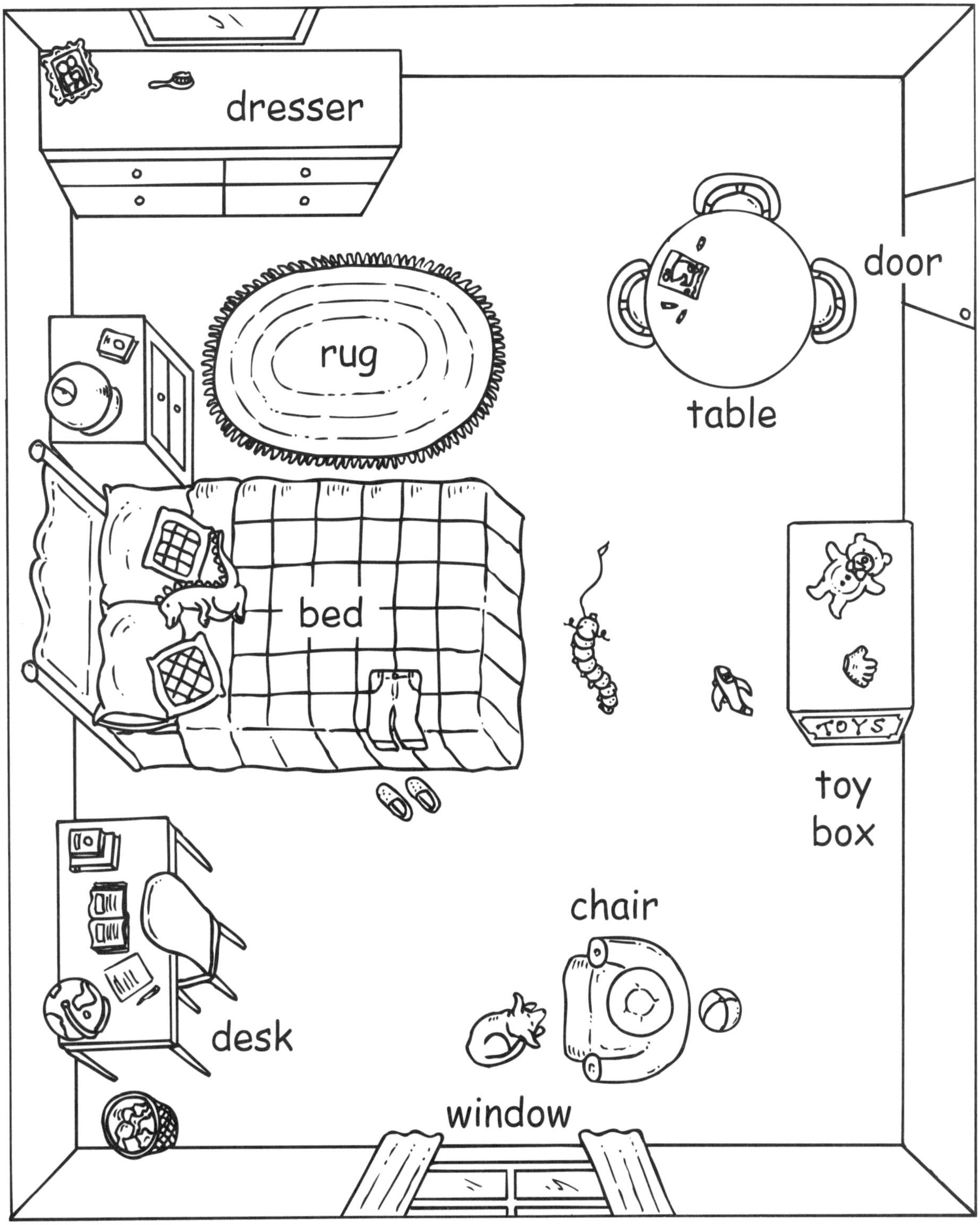

Name ______________________________

WEEK 1

What Is a Map?

Monday

1. A drawing of a place from above is a ________.

   bed map

2. The map shows Joey's ________.

   bedroom living room

Tuesday

1. What is on the bed?

2. What is on the toy box?

Wednesday

1. What is next to the rug?

bed

desk

2. What is next to the chair?

window

door

Name ____________________

Daily Geography

WEEK 1

What Is a Map?

Thursday

1. What is behind the chair?

2. What is in front of the chair?

Friday

1. Where does Joey sleep?

bed

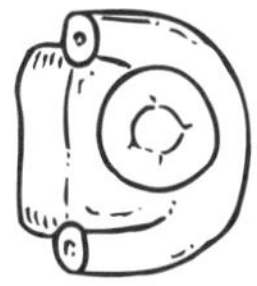
chair

2. Where does Joey color?

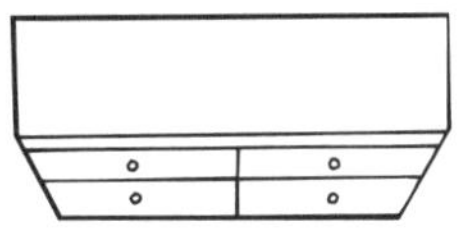
dresser

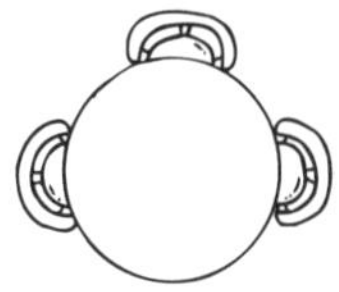
table

Challenge

Color your favorite place in Joey's bedroom.

WEEK 2

ANSWER KEY

Monday
1. places
2. classroom

Tuesday
1. teacher's desk
2. table

Wednesday
1. sink
2. computers

Thursday
1. books
2. teacher's desk

Friday
1. at the teacher's desk
2. at the sink

Challenge

Students should follow the teacher's directions to:
1. draw an apple on the teacher's desk,
2. color the computers yellow,
3. put an X on one of the desks,
4. color blue water in sink,
5. draw a pencil on table, and
6. color the reading rug brown.

Using a Map

Introducing the Map

Ask students to look around the classroom. Ask what kinds of things are found in the classroom. Students will probably say things like tables, chairs, desks, and computers.

Ask students to think about how they would draw a picture of the whole classroom with everything in it. Tell them that it would be easier to think about where things are if they were high above it. Then they could look down and see everything in its place.

Share with students that when they make a special picture like this, it is called a map. A map is a picture that shows where things are. A map looks like someone drew it from high above. Talk about how maps are useful.

Show students the map of Mr. Brown's classroom. Tell students to pretend they are high above this classroom. They are looking down on it. Talk about the things that are in the classroom and where they are found. Read the labels for students.

The questions for this map include the use of positional words. Positional words help describe the location or position of things on a map. The following words are used: *front/back, left/right,* and *near/far.* Talk about the directions by asking students to look for something on the map that corresponds with each positional word or pair of words.

In this lesson, students begin to develop a sense of direction. The skill of using positional words is included in this lesson. Weeks 1 and 3 also provide students practice with these skills.

Introducing Vocabulary

map

A map is a drawing of a place as seen from above.
A map shows where things are.

Mr. Brown's Classroom

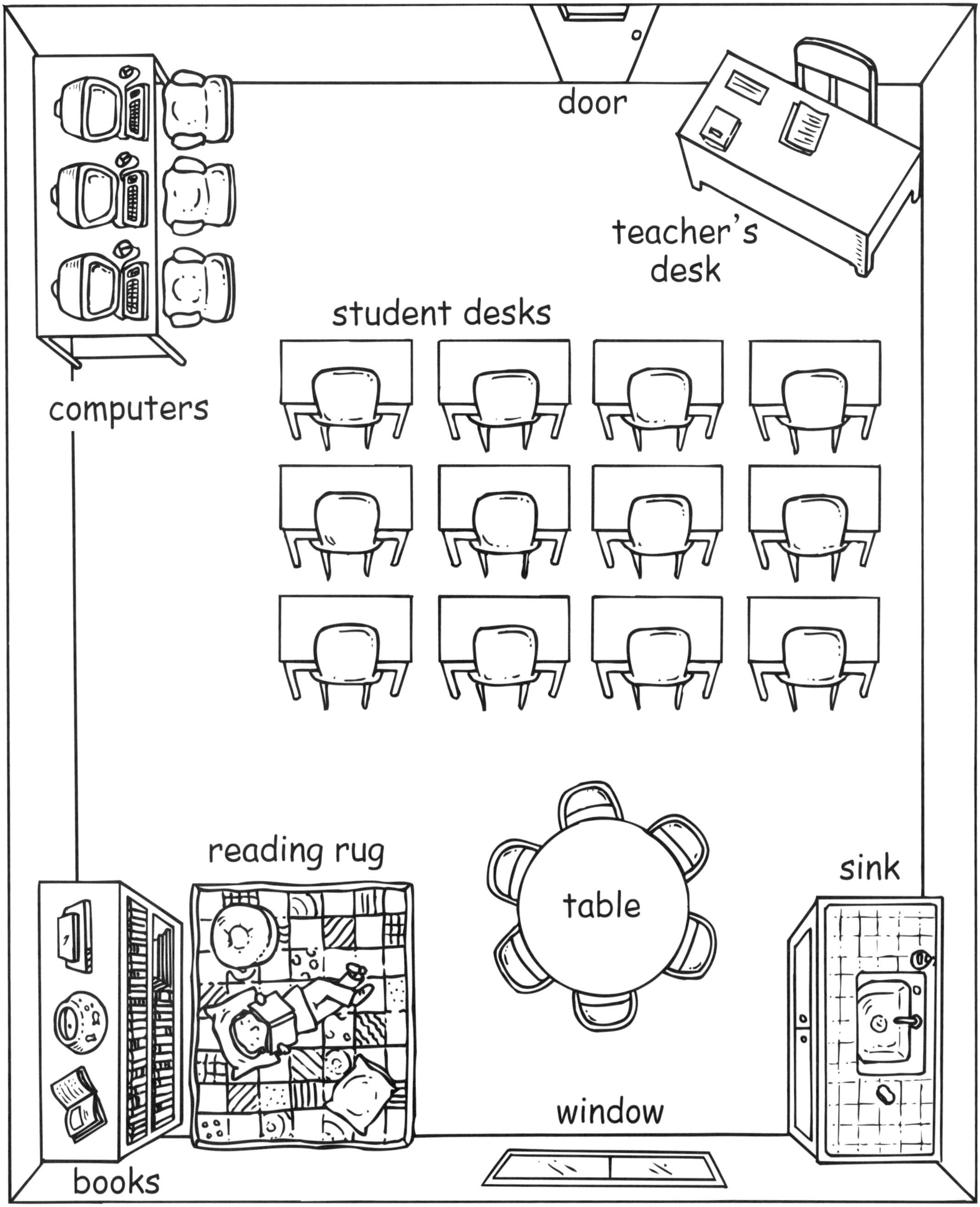

Name ______________________________

Daily Geography

WEEK 2

Using a Map

Monday

1. You use a map to find ________.

   friends places

2. The map shows Mr. Brown's ________.

   bedroom classroom

Tuesday

1. What is in the front of the classroom?

2. What is in the back of the classroom?

Wednesday

1. What is on the right side of the classroom?

2. What is on the left side of the classroom?

Name ____________________

Daily Geography

Using a Map

WEEK 2

Thursday

1. What is near the reading rug?

   books   computers

2. What is far away from the reading rug?

   table   teacher's desk

Friday

1. Where does Mr. Brown sit?

   at the sink   at the teacher's desk

2. Where does Mr. Brown wash his hands?

   at the computer   at the sink

Challenge

Follow directions to color the classroom map.

1. Draw an apple on the teacher's desk.
2. Color the three computers yellow.
3. Mark an X on your favorite student desk.
4. Color blue water in the sink.
5. Draw a pencil on the table.
6. Color the reading rug brown.

ANSWER KEY

Monday
1. live
2. homes

Tuesday
1. 3
2. 2B

Wednesday
1. 2A
2. below

Thursday
1. first
2. second

Friday
1. upstairs
2. downstairs

Challenge
Answers will vary, but students should:
1. name their favorite apartment,
2. name the floor it's on, and
3. color their favorite apartment.

Finding Places on a Map

Introducing the Map

Define *apartment* for students. Tell students that an apartment is one kind of home. Lots of people all over the world live in apartments. Ask if any of the students live in one or have a relative or friend that does. Talk about how some apartment buildings are small, while others may be very large. Apartments may have a few families or many families, depending on the size of the building.

Show students the map of the apartment building called Garden Apartments. Read the caption at the top of the page to help students understand what an apartment building map shows. Help students understand that they are looking right into the apartment building. This cutaway helps to show students the three floors of apartments. Talk about the ordinal numbers—*first, second,* and *third*—as you discuss the three floors. Talk about the different families that live on each floor. Help students notice that apartment 2B is empty. Read the sign in front and explain what the phrase "for rent" means.

Besides ordinal numbers, the questions for this map also include the use of positional words. Positional words describe a location or position. The following positional words are used on the map questions: *above/below* and *upstairs/downstairs.*

In this lesson, students begin to develop a sense of direction. The skills of ordinals and positional words are included in this lesson. Weeks 1 and 2 also provide students practice with positional words.

Introducing Vocabulary

apartment
An apartment is a set of rooms to live in.
Apartments are in a big building.

floor
A floor is the story of a building.
A three-story building has 3 floors.

map
A map shows where things are.
A map can show where people live.

Name

Finding Places on a Map

This map shows an apartment building.
Apartments are homes for people.
This map shows where people live.

Name ___________________________

Daily Geography

WEEK 3

Finding Places on a Map

Monday

1. The map shows where people ________.

   live　　　　work

2. Apartments are ________.

   cars　　　　homes

Tuesday

1. How many floors are there?

   1　　　　2　　　　3

2. Which apartment is for rent?

   2A　　　　2B　　　　2C

Wednesday

1. What apartment is above the Guzmans?

   2A　　　　2B　　　　2C

2. The Wongs live ________ Mr. and Mrs. Young.

   above　　　　below

Name ______________________________

Daily Geography

WEEK 3

Finding Places on a Map

Thursday

1. 1A is on the ________ floor.

   first second third

2. The Wongs live on the ________ floor.

   first second third

Friday

1. The Johnsons live ________.

   downstairs upstairs

2. Ms. Carter lives ________.

   downstairs upstairs

Challenge

1. In which apartment would you like to live? ____________

2. What floor is it on? ______________

3. Color your favorite apartment.

WEEK 4

Daily Geography

ANSWER KEY

Monday
1. school
2. 4

Tuesday
1. north
2. south

Wednesday
1. east
2. west

Thursday
1. bikes
2. flag

Friday
1. sandbox
2. playground

Challenge
1. north, south, east, and west
2. Students should circle the four direction arrows on the map.

Directions on a Map

Introducing the Map

Before starting the lesson, make four large direction cards. Place the four cards on the board in the correct positions. Tell students that there are four words that are called directions. They are *north, south, east,* and *west.* They are used to find places. Tell students that on a map north points up and south points down. East is on the right side and west is on the left side. Have students practice pointing north, south, east, and west.

Show students the map of Franklin School. Point out the four directions that are written on the map. North is at the top of the map, and south is at the bottom of the map. East is on the right side, and west is on the left side of the map.

Talk about how these four directions help them to find places on the map. For example, the swings are found on the east side of the school grounds. Find other places or things on the map. Ask students where they are found.

Help students to understand that when they are finding things on a map, they start at one place. For example, have students look at the school building. Then ask a question based on that starting point, "The cars are what direction from the school building?" They should answer that the cars are east of the school building. Since this is a difficult skill, ask students several more of these kinds of questions to check for understanding.

In Week 5, students will practice using a compass rose to find directions. A compass rose is found on most maps.

Introducing Vocabulary

direction

A direction tells where something is found.
The four main directions are north, south, east, and west.

Name

Directions on a Map

This map shows a school. This map has directions on it. The directions are north, south, east, and west.

Name ______________________________

Daily Geography

WEEK 4

Directions on a Map

Monday

1. The map shows a ________.

    bedroom   school

2. How many directions are on the map?

    1   2   3   4

Tuesday

1. Which direction points up?

    north   south

2. Which direction points down?

    north   south

Wednesday

1. Which direction points right?

    east   west

2. Which direction points left?

    east   west

Name ________________________________

Daily Geography

WEEK 4

Directions on a Map

Thursday

1. What is north of the swing set?

   bikes slide

2. What is east of the tree?

   flag sandbox

Friday

1. What is west of the sidewalk?

   sandbox swing set

2. What is south of Franklin School?

   parking lot playground

Challenge

1. What are the four main directions?

   ______________ ______________

   ______________ ______________

2. Circle the four direction arrows on the map.

WEEK 5

Daily Geography

ANSWER KEY

Monday
1. zoo
2. 4

Tuesday
1. S
2. E

Wednesday
1. west
2. north

Thursday
1. horse
2. turtles

Friday
1. pigs
2. ducks

Challenge

Students should follow the teacher's directions to:

1. color the cow black and white,
2. color the horse brown,
3. color the turtles green,
4. color the ducks yellow,
5. color the rabbits tan,
6. color the sheep white, and
7. color the pigs pink.

Using Directions

Introducing the Map

Tell students that maps show directions. On a map, north is toward the top. South is toward the bottom. To the right is east and to the left is west. Share with students that many maps that they see show the four main directions with a compass rose.

Show students the map of the zoo. Read the caption and point out the compass rose. Share with students that only the first letter of each direction is used. The letter *N* stands for north, *S* stands for south, *E* stands for east, and *W* stands for west.

Look at the petting zoo animals with the students. Name the animals and talk about where they are located in the zoo. Use the cow as the starting point when you ask students a couple of directional questions. For example, "Which animals are east of the cow?" Students should look at the compass rose. They will see that E (east) is to the right. Students can then look to the right of the cow to find the turtles. The turtles are east of the cow. Ask other questions using directions to check for understanding.

In this lesson, students get practice using the four main directions. They learn that most maps have a compass rose that shows these directions. Students are not expected to define the term *compass rose,* but rather begin to recognize a compass rose on a map and understand that it shows directions. They also learn that letters can stand for the four directions on a map.

Introducing Vocabulary

direction

A direction tells where something is found.
The four main directions are north, south, east, and west.

compass rose

A compass rose is a symbol on a map.
It shows directions such as north, south, east, and west.

Using Directions

This is a compass rose.

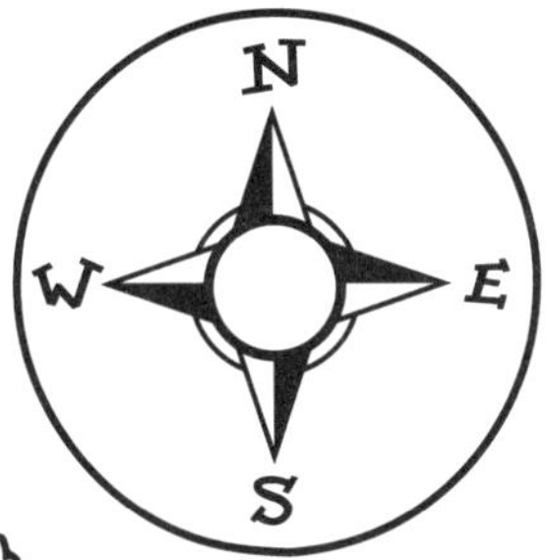

- The letter **N** stands for north.
- The letter **S** stands for south.
- The letter **E** stands for east.
- The letter **W** stands for west.

Name ____________________

Daily Geography

WEEK 5

Using Directions

Monday

1. The map shows a ________.

park zoo

2. The compass rose shows ________ directions.

2 4

Tuesday

1. What letter stands for south?

N S

2. What letter stands for east?

E W

Wednesday

1. The letter **W** stands for ________.

east west

2. The letter **N** stands for ________.

north south

Name ________________________________

Daily Geography

WEEK 5

Using Directions

Thursday

1. What is **N** of the cow?

   horse   sheep

2. What is **E** of the cow?

   rabbits   turtles

Friday

1. What is **W** of the sheep? ____________________

2. What is **N** of the turtles? ____________________

Challenge

1. Color the cow black and white.
2. Color the animal north of the cow brown.
3. Color the animals that are east of the cow green.
4. Color the animals that are north and east of the cow yellow.
5. Color the animals that are north and west of the cow tan.
6. Color the animals that are south and east of the cow white.
7. Color the animals that are south and west of the cow pink.

WEEK 6

Daily Geography

ANSWER KEY

Monday

1. Pinewood Springs
2. 

   hill

Tuesday

1. 
2. 

Wednesday

1. 
2. 

Thursday

1. 
2. 

Friday

1. mountain
2. plain

Challenge

Students should draw a tree and write the word *woods* on the map key.

A Map Key

Introducing the Map

Show students the map of Pinewood Springs. Talk about how this map shows the land and water of Pinewood Springs. Tell students this is a vacation spot in a mountainous area. Point out the cabin and discuss how fun it would be to stay in this cabin. Also, talk about the compass rose and how it shows the four directions on the map.

Ask students to name other things they see. Then share with students that there are some things on the map, and that you are not sure what they are. Tell them you know how you can find out. You can look at the map key. Tell students that maps use pictures to show real things. Mapmakers use a map key to tell what those pictures stand for. Point out the map key and read the caption to the students. Look at the small pictures. Those pictures are called symbols. Each picture has a word to tell what it stands for. Read and discuss the different symbols they see on the map key. Define the physical features for students. Have students look at the symbol for mountain. Then have them find all the mountains on the map. Talk about the other physical features on the map key and on the map.

In this lesson, students are introduced to a map key. Students will also practice using a map key in Week 7. Map keys are used throughout the rest of the book. Note that students are not expected to define the physical features at this time, but they are included for your reference. Physical maps are featured in more depth during Weeks 13–18.

Introducing Vocabulary

hill

A hill is land that rises above the land around it.
It is not as high as a mountain.

lake

A lake is a body of water with land all around it.

map key

A map key shows the symbols on a map.
It tells what each symbol stands for.

mountain

A mountain is land that rises very high above the land around it.
It is higher than a hill.

plain

A plain is flat land.

river

A river is a large stream of water that flows across the land.

symbol

A symbol is a drawing that stands for something real.

A Map Key

This map has a key. A map key has symbols.
The symbols are drawings. They stand for real things.

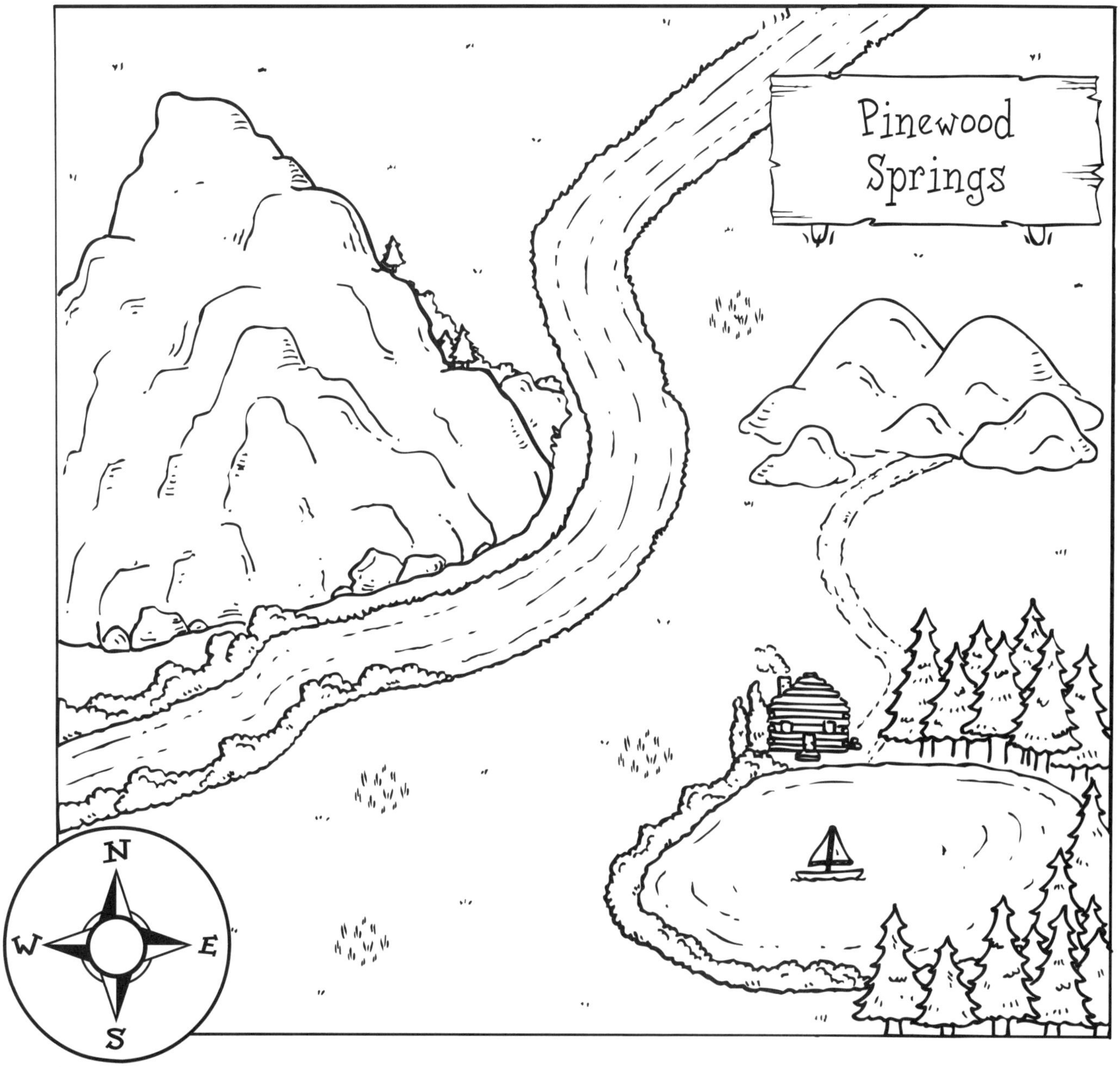

Map Key

 mountain  river  hill

 lake  plain

Name ______________________________

Daily Geography

WEEK 6

A Map Key

Monday

1. What is the name of the map?

Pinewood Springs   Rocky Point

2. Which one is on the map key?

hill

Tuesday

1. Which symbol stands for mountain?

2. Which symbol stands for river?

Wednesday

1. Which symbol stands for hill?

2. Which symbol stands for plain?

Name ______________________________

A Map Key

Thursday

1. What is south of the hills?  

2. What is west of the lake?  

Friday

1. Which one is the highest?

   hill mountain plain

2. Which one is the lowest?

   hill mountain plain

Challenge

The cabin is near trees. They are called woods. Draw a tree on the map key. Write the word **woods** by the tree.

WEEK 7

Daily Geography

ANSWER KEY

Monday

1. Lake View Park
2. 4

Tuesday

1. 
2. 

Wednesday

1. 
2. 

Thursday

1. camp
2. bear

Friday

1. north and east
2. lake

Challenge

Students should draw a picture of a cave in the map key and write the word **cave** next to it.

Using a Map Key

Introducing the Map

Show students the map of Lake View Park. This is a nature park where people are allowed to camp. Talk about the kinds of activities at a nature park. Point out the compass rose and tell students that it has letters that stand for north, south, east, and west. The compass rose helps find places on the map.

Tell students that this map has something else. It is called a map key. Tell students that maps use pictures to show real things. Mapmakers use a map key to tell what those pictures stand for. Point out the map key and read the caption to the students. Look at the small pictures. Those pictures are called symbols. Each picture has a word to tell what it stands for. Read and discuss the different symbols they see on the map key.

Instruct students to find the symbol for a camp. Students will see that a tent stands for a camp. Have students locate the camp on the map. Then have students find the symbol for a trail, or a path. Have students follow the trail on the map with a pointer finger. They will see that the trail goes by both the lake and the woods. Talk about the lake and the woods. The symbol for woods is a tree. Help students understand that the group of trees in the northern part of the park is the woods.

Week 6 introduced the concept of a map key. In this lesson, students get practice using a map key. Map keys are used throughout the book for additional practice.

Introducing Vocabulary

camp
A camp is an outdoor place with tents.

lake
A lake is a body of water with land all around it.

map key
A map key shows the symbols on a map.
It tells what each symbol stands for.

symbol
A symbol is a drawing that stands for something real.

trail
A trail is a path you follow.

woods
Woods is a small area with many trees.

Name

Using a Map Key

This map has a key. A map key has symbols. The symbols are drawings. They stand for real things.

Map Key

 camp  lake  trail  woods

Name ______________________________

Daily Geography

WEEK 7

Using a Map Key

Monday

1. What is the name of the map?

   Lake View Park   The Camp

2. How many symbols are on the map key?

   2   4

Tuesday

1. Which symbol stands for lake?  

2. Which symbol stands for camp?  

Wednesday

1. Which symbol stands for woods?  

2. What is next to the camp?  

Name ______________________________

Daily Geography

WEEK 7

Using a Map Key

Thursday

1. What is south of the lake?

   camp   woods

2. What is east of the camp?

   bear   ducks

Friday

1. The woods are ________ of the trail.

   north and east   north and west

2. You follow the trail to the ________________.

Challenge

1. Find the bear in a cave.
2. Draw a cave on the map key.
3. Write the word **cave** by your symbol.

WEEK 8

ANSWER KEY

Monday

1. Maria's Neighborhood
2. map key

Tuesday

1. 
2. 

Wednesday

1. High
2. 

Thursday

1. 
2. 

Friday

1. park
2. Main Street

Challenge

Students should follow the teacher's directions to:

1. circle the title,
2. outline the key in red, and
3. color the compass rose yellow.

Parts of a Map

Introducing the Map

Students have been introduced to directions and a map key in previous lessons. Tell students that most maps have three things on them—a title, directions, and a map key. Define these terms for students.

Show students the map of the neighborhood. Read the title together and ask students what the map is about. It is about Maria's neighborhood. The map shows the places in her neighborhood. Read the street names for students. Next, look at the map key. Talk about how each symbol stands for a place on the map. Have students locate different places on the map. Point out the entrance to each place. Explain that each entrance leads to a street. The entrance tells on which street each building is found. For example, say, "Maria's house is on High Street."

Discuss the compass rose on the map and what each letter stands for. You may wish to have students write out *north, south, east,* and *west* in the correct positions on the map. Have students use the directions to find places on the map. For example, ask, "What is south of Maria's house?" (fire station)

In this lesson, students learn that there are basic parts of most maps. These include a title, a compass rose, and a map key. These basic elements of a map are used throughout the book for additional practice.

Introducing Vocabulary

compass rose
A compass rose is a symbol on a map.
It shows directions such as north, south, east, and west.

direction
A direction tells where something is found.
The four main directions are north, south, east, and west.

map key
A map key shows the symbols on a map.
It tells what each symbol stands for.

neighborhood
A neighborhood is a small area in a city where people live.

street
A street is a road in a town or city.
Most streets have buildings on both sides.

symbol
A symbol is a drawing that stands for something real.

title
A title is the name of the map.
It tells what the map is about.

Name

Parts of a Map

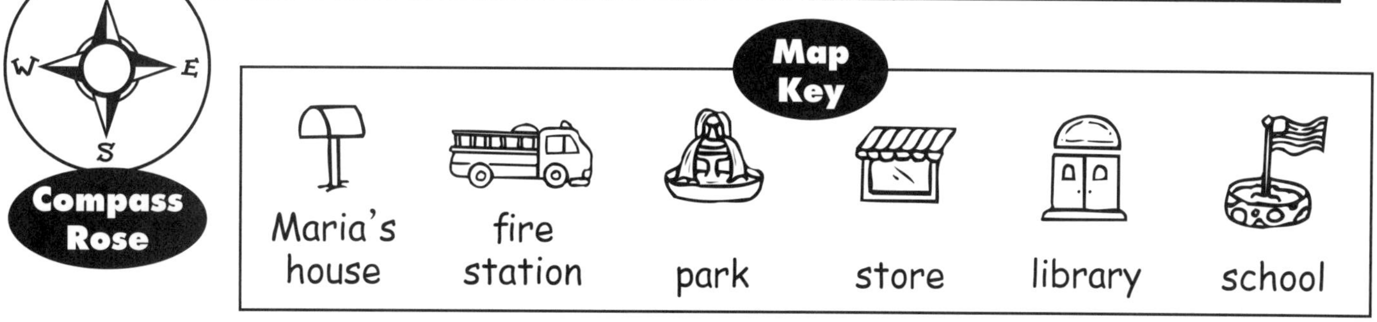

Name ____________________

Daily Geography

WEEK 8

Parts of a Map

Monday

1. The title of the map is ______.

   Fire Station   Maria's Neighborhood

2. A map has a title, a compass rose, and a

   ____

Tuesday

1. Which symbol stands for the school?

2. Which symbol stands for Maria's house?

Wednesday

1. Maria lives on ______ Street.

   Low   High

2. What is on Safe Street?  

Name ______________________________

Parts of a Map

Thursday

1. What is east of Maria's house?  

2. What is south of the library?  

Friday

1. What is on Safe Street and Low Street?

   library park

2. What runs north and south?

   Low Street Main Street

Challenge

1. Circle the title of the map.
2. Outline the map key in red.
3. Color the compass rose yellow.

WEEK 9

Daily Geography

ANSWER KEY

Monday
1. backyard
2. outside

Tuesday
1. yes
2. yes

Wednesday
1. 3
2. sandbox

Thursday
1. dog
2. swing set

Friday
1. treehouse
2. bike

Challenge
Answers will vary, but students should draw one thing from the backyard. The teacher may also choose the item(s) students should draw.

Picturing a Place

Introducing the Map

Ask students to look around the classroom for one minute. Tell them you are going to ask them to name things in the classroom later on, so they should really pay attention to different areas of the room. After one minute, have students close their eyes. Describe the classroom to students while their eyes are closed. Ask them to picture in their minds what their classroom looks like.

Ask students to open their eyes and look around the classroom again. Then tell students to close their eyes once more. Ask them to name things in the classroom. Have students open their eyes and look around the room. What did they remember? Explain to students that what they just did was to make a mental picture of the classroom. They made a map of the classroom in their minds.

Ask students to think about their home. Ask them to picture in their minds the inside and outside of their home. Where is the kitchen, their bedroom, or a bathroom? Have them think about the outside of their home. What kinds of things are outside? Tell students they have just made a picture in their minds of their home. They have just made a map of their home in their minds.

Now, have students look at the map of Joey's backyard. Talk about the different areas of his yard. Read the caption at the top of the page and have students follow the directions. Then have students open their eyes and turn the map over. Ask students which things they remembered about Joey's backyard. On the board, make a list of everything they remembered. Then have students turn the map back over to see how many things they remembered. Did they also remember where things were located?

Tell students that they made a map of Joey's backyard in their minds. Share with students that it is important to make pictures in their minds. Those pictures help them to remember better.

Students may find it difficult to understand the concept of mental maps. Students are not expected to define a mental map, but rather begin to understand how making pictures in their minds helps them to remember where things are located.

Introducing Vocabulary

mental map (not included in the glossary)
A mental map is a map that you picture in your mind.

Picturing a Place

This is a map of Joey's backyard. Look at it for one minute. Now close your eyes. Think of Joey's backyard. Open your eyes. You made a picture in your mind.

Name ___________________________________

Daily Geography

WEEK 9

Picturing a Place

Monday

1. The map shows Joey's ________.

   backyard   school

2. Joey's backyard is ________.

   inside   outside

Tuesday

1. Is there a treehouse?   yes   no

2. Is there a table?   yes   no

Wednesday

1. How many swings are there?

   1   2   3

2. What is by the tree?

   sandbox   table

Name ____

Daily Geography

Picturing a Place

WEEK 9

Thursday

1. Joey has a ________.

   cat dog

2. What is east of the garden?

   sandbox swing set

Friday

1. What is north of the doghouse?

   table treehouse

2. What is <u>not</u> in Joey's backyard?

   bike sandbox

Challenge

Look at Joey's backyard for one minute. Close your eyes. Think about Joey's backyard. Now open your eyes. Turn the map over so you can't see it. Draw one thing from Joey's backyard.

WEEK 10

Picturing the United States

Introducing the Map

Ask students to think about their house. Ask them to picture in their minds the inside of their house. Tell them that it helps to close their eyes when they picture something in their minds. Then tell students what they have just done is to make a map of their house.

Next, have them think about the neighborhood where they live. Have them take a "walk" through their neighborhood by thinking about the places near their homes. They have just made a map of their neighborhood in their minds—a mental map.

Now, ask them to think about something very large—the United States. Show students the large map of the U.S. in your classroom. Trace over the outline of the country with your finger. Then show students the map of the United States from the book. Talk about the shape of the U.S. Have them trace the outline shape of the country with their fingers.

Talk about how the United States is made up of 50 states. Tell students that all the states together make one big country. Most of the states are close together. Two states—Alaska and Hawaii—are far away from the others. That is why they have to be in little maps. Help students find their state within the country. Talk about how their state is a part of the country. Help students notice that each state is a different shape and size. What shape and size is their state?

In this lesson, students take a look at the United States. They look at the size and shape of the country. They also begin to recognize their state and its location within the United States.

Students may find it difficult to understand the concept of mental maps and may need a review each day. Students are not expected to define a mental map, but rather begin to understand how making pictures in their minds helps them to remember where things are located and what they look like.

Introducing Vocabulary

country

A country is a land and the people who live there.
The United States is a country.

mental map (not included in glossary)

A mental map is a map that you picture in your mind.

state

A state is part of a country.
There are 50 states in the United States.

ANSWER KEY

Monday
1. Picturing the United States
2. all

Tuesday
1. large
2. 50 states

Wednesday
1. North Dakota
2. Texas

Thursday
1. east
2. west

Friday
1. Alaska
2. west

Challenge
Students should write the name of their state and color their state on the map.

Name

Picturing the United States

The United States is a large country.
It has 50 states.

Name ______________________________

Daily Geography

WEEK 10

Picturing the United States

Monday

1. The title of the map is ________.

   Our Country　　　　Picturing the United States

2. The map shows ________ of the United States.

   all　　　　part

Tuesday

1. The United States is ________.

   large　　　　small

2. The map shows ________.

   1 state　　　　50 states

Wednesday

1. Which state is in the north?

   North Dakota　　　　Texas

2. Which state is in the south?

   North Dakota　　　　Texas

Name ______________________________

Daily Geography

WEEK 10

Picturing the United States

Thursday

1. Virginia is in the ________.

    east west

2. California is in the ________.

    east west

Friday

1. Which is larger?

    Alaska Hawaii

2. The larger states are in the ________.

    east west

Challenge

What is the name of your state?

____

Color your state on the map.

WEEK 11

Daily Geography

A Treasure Map

Introducing the Map

An important geography skill is looking at a map and finding the best route to take. In this lesson, students will listen to a follow-along map story. They will follow a route to find the treasure.

Show students the treasure map. Talk about how pirates used to bury treasure. Sometimes they buried it on an island so no one would find the treasure. They often left a map so they could come back and find the treasure. Point out some of the dangers on the island and the compass rose. Tell students you are going to tell them a story about Pete the Pirate. They need to look at the treasure map to follow Pete as he looks for his treasure.

Read the following story to students:

> Pete was a pirate. He sailed to the south end of an island. He was hunting for his treasure. Pete took out his map to help him. Pete began to follow the treasure map. He started by the two palm trees at the south end of the island. Pete walked slowly, counting his steps along the way. He went between a dead tree and a hut. Pete remembered the hut. He had hidden in there before.
>
> Pete headed north to a cave. He crawled into the cave. The cave was dark, and two yellow eyes stared at him. He raced out. In front of him was a volcano. Hot lava was running down the sides. Pete turned east, and staring right at him was a poisonous snake. Pete stood still for five whole minutes. The snake grew tired and slithered away. Pete could see two large palm trees ahead of him to the north and east. He looked at his map. There was a big "X" on the map. The "X" was between the two trees. This is where he had hidden his treasure. Pete took four giant steps. He started digging in the sand between the two trees. What did Pete the Pirate find?

Ask students to name things Pete could have found in his treasure chest. Tell students that this map helped Pete follow a path, or a route, to the treasure. Remind students that maps are useful to help find their way along a route.

Introducing Vocabulary

island

An island is land with water all around it.

route

A route is a way to go from one place to another.

ANSWER KEY

Monday
1. treasure map
2. an island

Tuesday
1. route
2. path

Wednesday
1. south
2. cave

Thursday
1. 
2. snake

Friday
1. 
2. north

Challenge
1. Students should trace the route from "Start here" to the X.
2. Students should draw a treasure chest near the X on the map.

Name

A Treasure Map

This is Pete's map.
He is looking for treasure.
Which way should he go?
Follow the route.

Name ______________________________

Daily Geography

WEEK 11

A Treasure Map

Monday

1. What kind of map is it?

   neighborhood map   treasure map

2. The map shows ________.

   an island   a sailboat

Tuesday

1. Pete followed a ________.

   route   street

2. A route is a ________.

   direction   path

Wednesday

1. Pete started in the ________ part of the island.

   north   south

2. Pete went through a ________.

cave

hut

Name ______________________________

Daily Geography

WEEK 11

A Treasure Map

Thursday

1. What is north of the cave?  

2. Pete saw a ________ on his route.

   bear   snake

Friday

1. Where is the treasure?  

2. The treasure is on the ________ side of the island.

   north   south

Challenge

1. Trace Pete's route to the treasure.
2. Draw a chest where the treasure is buried.

WEEK 12

Daily Geography

ANSWER KEY

Monday
1. A Street Map
2. neighborhood

Tuesday
1. 2
2. First

Wednesday
1. Third
2. Green

Thursday
1. Brown Street
2. Second Street

Friday
1. Third Street
2. Kim

Challenge
Students should color Kari's house yellow and the school red. They should draw a route from Kari's house to school using a black crayon. The most direct route would be: start at Kari's house on First Street; turn south on Green Street; and then go east onto Third Street to get to the school.

A Street Map

Introducing the Map

Ask students to name the street on which they live. Talk about how there are other words for *street* such as *avenue, road, lane,* and *way.* Tell students that no matter what the streets are called, they are all routes. Define *route* for students and tell students your route from your home to school each day, pointing out the streets you travel. Have one or more students explain his or her route to school.

Show students the street map of a neighborhood. Explain that this map shows where Kari and Kim live. Point out their houses. Have students trace the streets in this area. Talk about the different buildings on each street. Talk about how important it is to read a street map to find different places. People can get mixed up if they don't follow a street map.

Ask students where the fire station is located. Help them understand that it is on First Street, because the driveway opens up onto that street. For more advanced study, you may want to talk about how the fire station is located at the corner of First Street and Brown Street. Ask about other locations on the map.

Ask students which way Kari should go to school. Have the students follow her route. Kari would start at First Street; turn south on Green Street; and then turn east onto Third Street. Ask students about other routes that Kari and her friend Kim could take to get to other places in their neighborhood. The students will be asked again to follow Kari's route to school on the challenge question.

In this lesson, students begin to understand how to follow a route on a street map. Other community maps that include streets are included in this book for further practice.

Introducing Vocabulary

neighborhood
A neighborhood is a small area in a city where people live.

route
A route is a way to go from one place to another.

street
A street is a road in a town or city.
Most streets have buildings on both sides.

Name

A Street Map

This is Kari's neighborhood. She wants to go to school. Which route should she take? Which way should she go?

Name ______________________________

Daily Geography

WEEK 12

A Street Map

Monday

1. What is the title of the map?

   Kari's House   A Street Map

2. The map shows a ________.

   neighborhood   state

Tuesday

1. There are ________ houses in the neighborhood.

   2   8

2. Kari and Kim live on ________ Street.

   First   Second

Wednesday

1. The hospital is on ________ Street.

   Second   Third

2. The gas station is on ________ Street.

   Green   Brown

Name ____

Daily Geography

WEEK 12

A Street Map

Thursday

1. Which street runs north and south?

   Brown Street		First Street

2. Which street runs east and west?

   Green Street		Second Street

Friday

1. The park is <u>not</u> on ________.

   First Street		Third Street

2. Who lives across the street from the park?

   Kim		Kari

Challenge

1. Color Kari's house yellow.
2. Color the school red.
3. Draw Kari's route from home to school in black.

WEEK 13

Daily Geography

ANSWER KEY

Monday
1. Earth
2. round

Tuesday
1. both land and water
2. both land and water

Wednesday
1. continents
2. oceans

Thursday
1. North or South
2. Atlantic or Pacific

Friday
1. Atlantic Ocean
2. Pacific Ocean

Challenge
Students should color the continents green and the oceans blue.

Skill: Physical Features — Essential Element 2: Standard 4

What Is a Globe?

Introducing the Map

Show students the classroom globe. Tell students that a globe shows Earth. Explain to students that the Earth is very large. Tell them that a globe is a small model used to show the whole Earth. Like Earth, a globe is round, or shaped like a ball. The globe shows Earth's largest land and water areas. The largest land areas are called continents. The largest water areas are called oceans. Tell students that most of Earth is made up of oceans.

Show students the picture of the globe. Talk about the title. Ask students, "What is a globe?" Read the caption with students to answer the question.

Then talk about how a flat picture of a globe can only show one side of Earth. This globe shows the side that has two large areas of land. It shows two continents—North America and South America. The picture of the globe also shows two oceans—the Atlantic Ocean and the Pacific Ocean.

You may wish to extend the lesson to talk about how the United States, Canada, and Mexico are three of the countries in North America. You may also want to have students make a mental picture of where the United States is located within North America.

In this lesson, students are introduced to the globe. They see that Earth is made up of large land and water areas. In Week 14, students will look at a world map to see all the continents and oceans.

Introducing Vocabulary

continent
A continent is a large area of land.
North America is a continent.

Earth
Earth is the planet where we live.

globe
A globe is a model of Earth.

ocean
An ocean is a large body of water.
Earth has five oceans.

Name

What Is a Globe?

A globe is a model of Earth. It is round like Earth.

A globe shows the continents.
Continents are large areas of land.

A globe shows oceans. Oceans are large bodies of water.

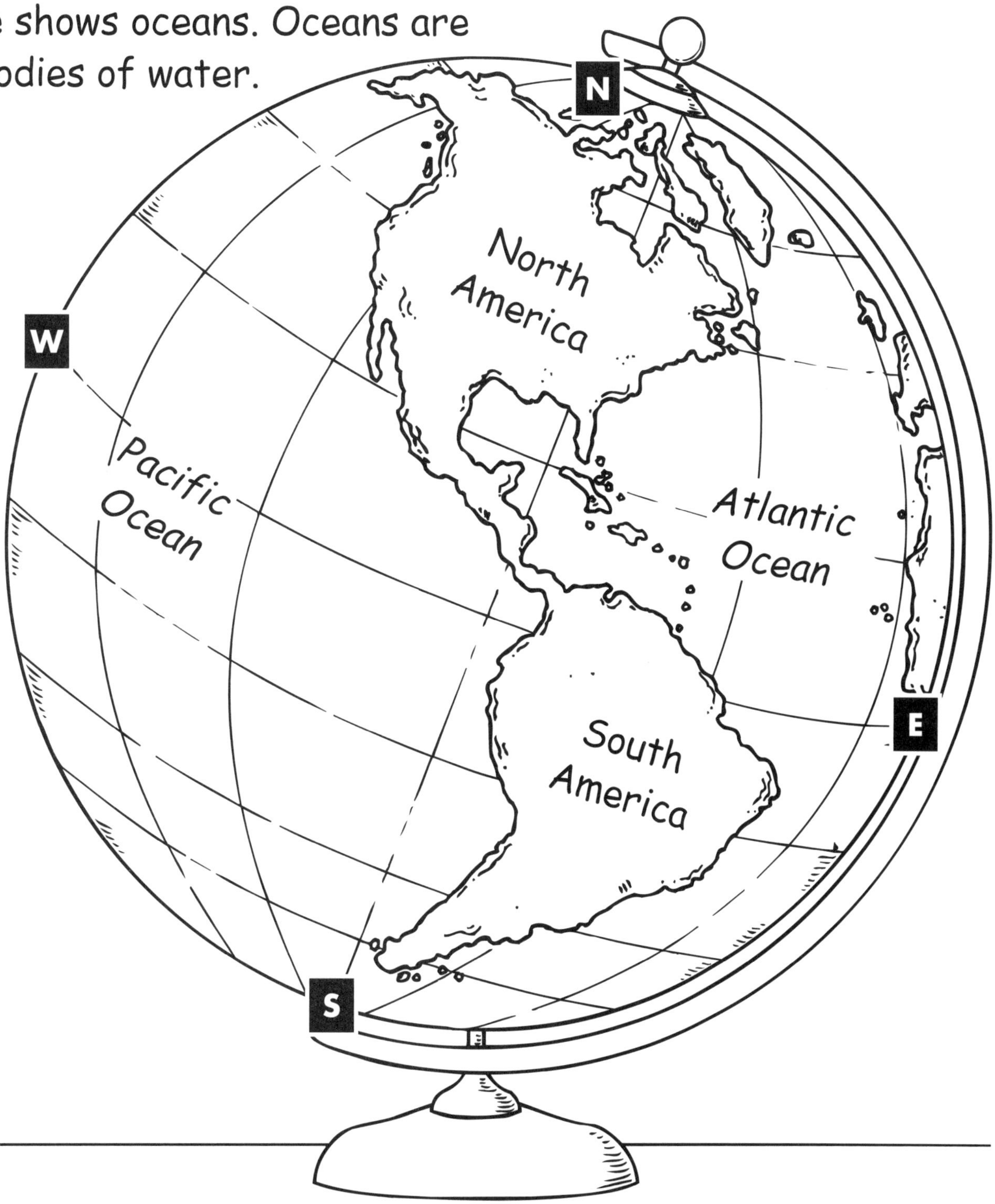

Name ______________________________

Daily Geography

WEEK 13

What Is a Globe?

Monday

1. A globe is a model of ________.

   Earth   Mars

2. Earth and a globe are both ________.

   round   square

Tuesday

1. The Earth has ________.

   only land   only water   both land and water

2. The globe shows ________.

   only land   only water   both land and water

Wednesday

1. Large areas of land are ________.

   continents   oceans

2. Large bodies of water are ________.

   continents   oceans

Name ______________________________

Daily Geography

WEEK 13

What Is a Globe?

Thursday

1. Name one continent on the picture of the globe.

    ______________________________ America

2. Name one ocean on the picture of the globe.

    ______________________________ Ocean

Friday

1. Which ocean is east of North America?

    ____

2. Which ocean is west of South America?

    ____

Challenge

Color the continents green. Color the oceans blue.

WEEK 14

Daily Geography

ANSWER KEY

Monday
1. all
2. water

Tuesday
1. 7
2. an animal

Wednesday
1. 5
2. 

Thursday
1. 
2. 

Friday
1. Arctic
2. south

Challenge
Students should circle their favorite animal on the map. Students should name the continent in which the animal lives.

A World Map

Introducing the Map

Show students the classroom globe. Talk about how the globe shows the world, or all of Earth. The globe shows the land and water on Earth. Then show students the classroom map of the world. Talk about how it is a flat picture of Earth. The world map shows all the land and water on Earth.

Show students the world map from the book. Talk about how the world is divided into seven large land areas called continents. Name and locate the seven continents of the world. Talk about the animal that represents each continent:

Africa/lion, Antarctica/penguin, Asia/water buffalo, Australia/kangaroo, Europe/bear, North America/moose, and South America/parrot. The animals will help students locate the different continents.

Discuss with students that the large water areas are called oceans. The world has five oceans—Arctic, Atlantic, Indian, Pacific, and Southern. Help the students name and locate the different oceans.

In this lesson, students are introduced to the world map. The world map shows the seven continents and the five oceans of the world. Continents and oceans are also discussed in Week 13.

Introducing Vocabulary

continent
A continent is a large area of land.
North America is a continent.

Earth
Earth is the planet where we live.

ocean
An ocean is a large body of water.
Earth has five oceans.

world
The world is another name for Earth.

Name

A World Map

The world has 7 large areas of land. They are called continents.
The world has 5 large bodies of water. They are called oceans.

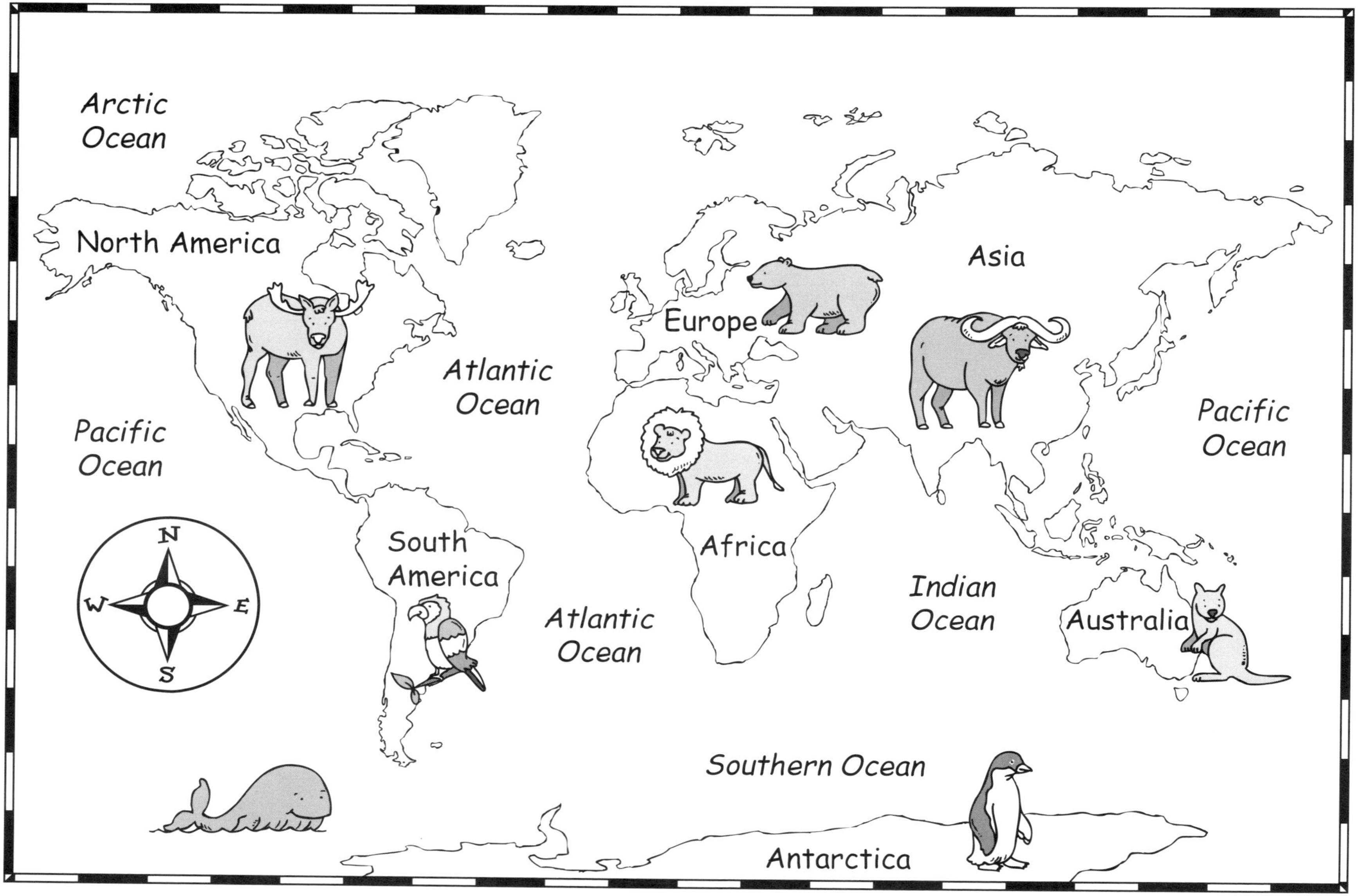

Name ______________________________

A World Map

WEEK 14

Monday

1. The map shows ________ of the world.

   all   part

2. The map shows land and ________.

   trees   water

Tuesday

1. There are ________ continents.

   4   7

2. Each continent shows ________.

   an animal   a tree

Wednesday

1. There are ________ oceans.

   5   7

2. A ________ is in the Pacific Ocean.

Name ______________________________

Daily Geography

WEEK 14

A World Map

Thursday

1. Which animal is on Africa?

2. Which animal is on South America?

Friday

1. The ________ Ocean is in the north.

   Arctic   Pacific

2. Antarctica is in the ________.

   north   south

Challenge

Circle your favorite animal on the map.

In which continent is it found?

____

WEEK 15

Daily Geography

ANSWER KEY

Monday

1. Colorado
2. water

Tuesday

1. 
2. 

Wednesday

1. 
2. 

Thursday

1. east
2. west

Friday

1. Rio Grande
2. Colorado River

Challenge

Students should color the mountains brown, the plains green, and the four rivers blue.

A Land and Water Map of Colorado

Introducing the Map

Share with students that some maps show cities. Other maps show things like mountains and rivers. Show students the map of Colorado. Tell them that this state map shows the kinds of land and water Colorado has. Look at the map key to see the symbol for each feature. Colorado is famous for its mountains. They are called the Rocky Mountains. Many people visit the Rocky Mountains to hike and ski. Look at the map to locate the areas of Colorado that are mountainous.

Talk about how the eastern part of Colorado is covered with plains. They are called the Great Plains. Tell students that plains are low flatlands that are good for farming and ranching.

Talk about the important rivers that are in Colorado. Name the rivers for students.

Tell students that the Colorado River is the most important one. Several states around Colorado get their water from the Colorado River.

In this lesson, students are introduced to three physical features—mountains, plains, and rivers. Weeks 16 through 18 highlight other physical features.

Introducing Vocabulary

mountain

A mountain is land that rises very high above the land around it. It is higher than a hill.

plain

A plain is flat land.

river

A river is a large stream of water that flows across the land.

A Land and Water Map of Colorado

Colorado has many mountains. The mountains are very high land. Colorado has plains. The plains are very low, flat land.

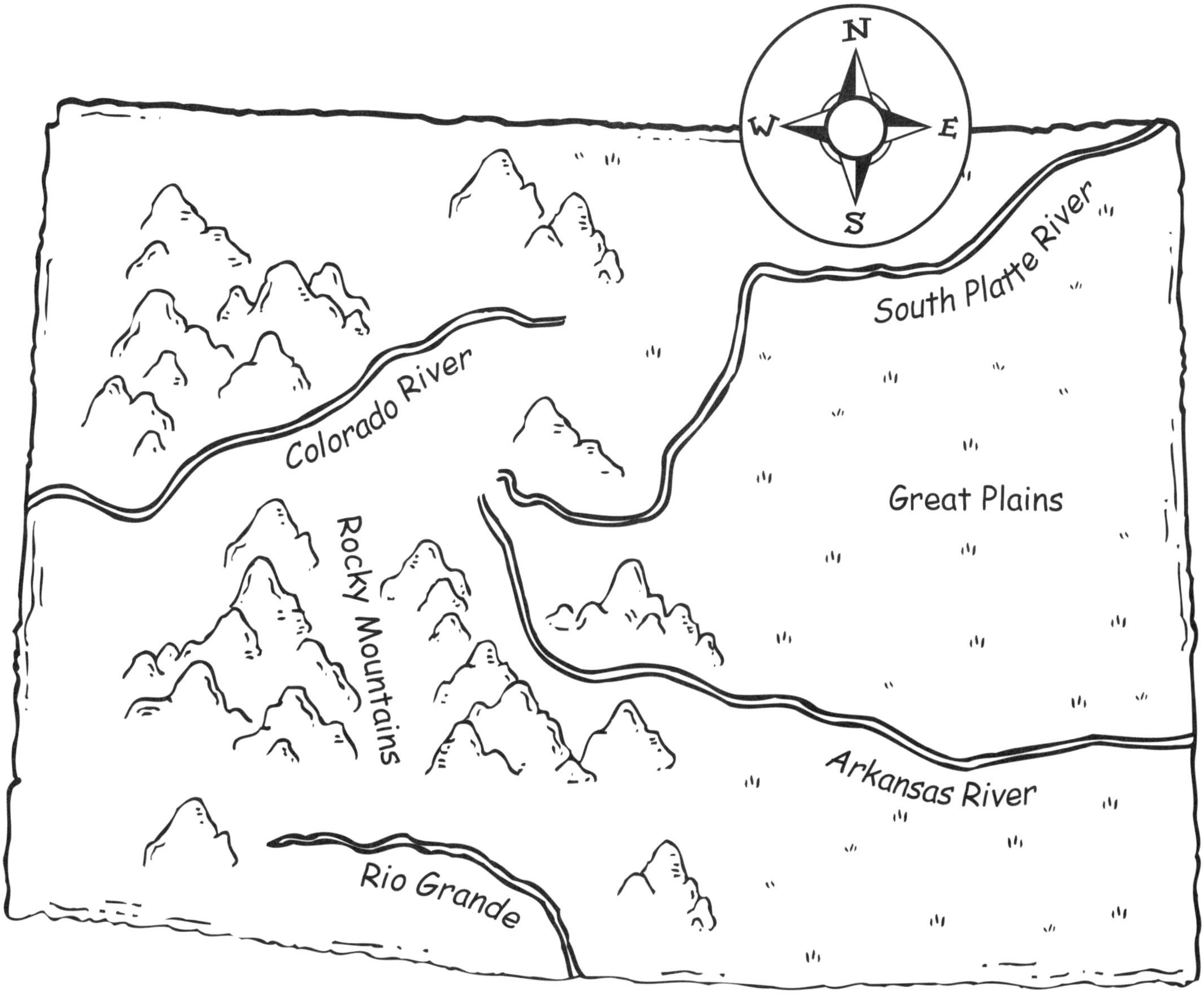

Map Key

Name ____

Daily Geography

WEEK 15

A Land and Water Map of Colorado

Monday

1. The map shows ________.

   Arizona   Colorado

2. The map shows land and ________.

   cities   water

Tuesday

1. Which symbol stands for a mountain?

2. Which symbol stands for plains?

Wednesday

1. What is very high land?

2. What is low, flat land?

Name ______________________________

Daily Geography

WEEK 15

A Land and Water Map of Colorado

Thursday

1. The Great Plains are in the ________.

    east   west

2. The Rocky Mountains are in the ________.

    east   west

Friday

1. Which river is in the south?

    Rio Grande   South Platte River

2. Which river has the same name as the state?

    Arkansas River   Colorado River

Challenge

1. Color the mountains brown.
2. Color the plains green.
3. Color the rivers blue.

WEEK 16

Daily Geography

ANSWER KEY

Monday

1. Arizona
2. water

Tuesday

1. 
2. 

Wednesday

1. Sonoran Desert
2. north

Thursday

1. Colorado
2. Gila River

Friday

1. land
2. water

Challenge

Students should color the Grand Canyon red, yellow, and brown. The deserts should be yellow, the mountains brown, and the rivers blue.

Skill: Physical Features | Essential Element 2: Standard 4

A Land and Water Map of Arizona

Introducing the Map

Share with students that some maps show just cities. Other maps show things like deserts, mountains, and rivers. Show students the map of Arizona. Tell them that this map shows the land and water in the state. Review the symbols on the map key with students.

Talk about the deserts of Arizona. After you have defined *desert* for students, have them look at the Painted Desert. It is known for its colorful rocks, and it is rocky. The Sonoran Desert in southern Arizona is hot and dry, but it gets short periods of heavy rains. Giant saguaro cactus plants grow there. The desert is made of gravel and sand. It also has rocky hills, and there are mountains in this area, too.

Arizona also has canyons. Define *canyon* for students. Tell students the most famous one is called Grand Canyon. The Grand Canyon is one of the largest canyons in the world. The Grand Canyon is about 1 mile (1.6 km) deep. It is 277 miles (446 km) long. Compare the length and depth of the canyon to local distances in your area, such as how far it is from one city to the next.

Two rivers are shown on the map—the Colorado and Gila (Hee la) Rivers. Talk about how the Colorado River runs at the bottom of the Grand Canyon. The Gila and Colorado Rivers meet in the southwest area of Arizona.

In this lesson, students are introduced to two new physical features—canyon and desert. Mountains and rivers were introduced in Week 15 and are represented on this map as well.

Introducing Vocabulary

canyon
A canyon is a deep valley with steep sides.

desert
A desert is a dry, sandy, or rocky area of land.

mountain
A mountain is land that rises very high above the land around it. It is higher than a hill.

river
A river is a large stream of water that flows across the land.

A Land and Water Map of Arizona

Arizona has deserts. The deserts are hot and dry. They are sandy and rocky. Arizona has a large canyon. The canyon is a deep valley. It has steep sides.

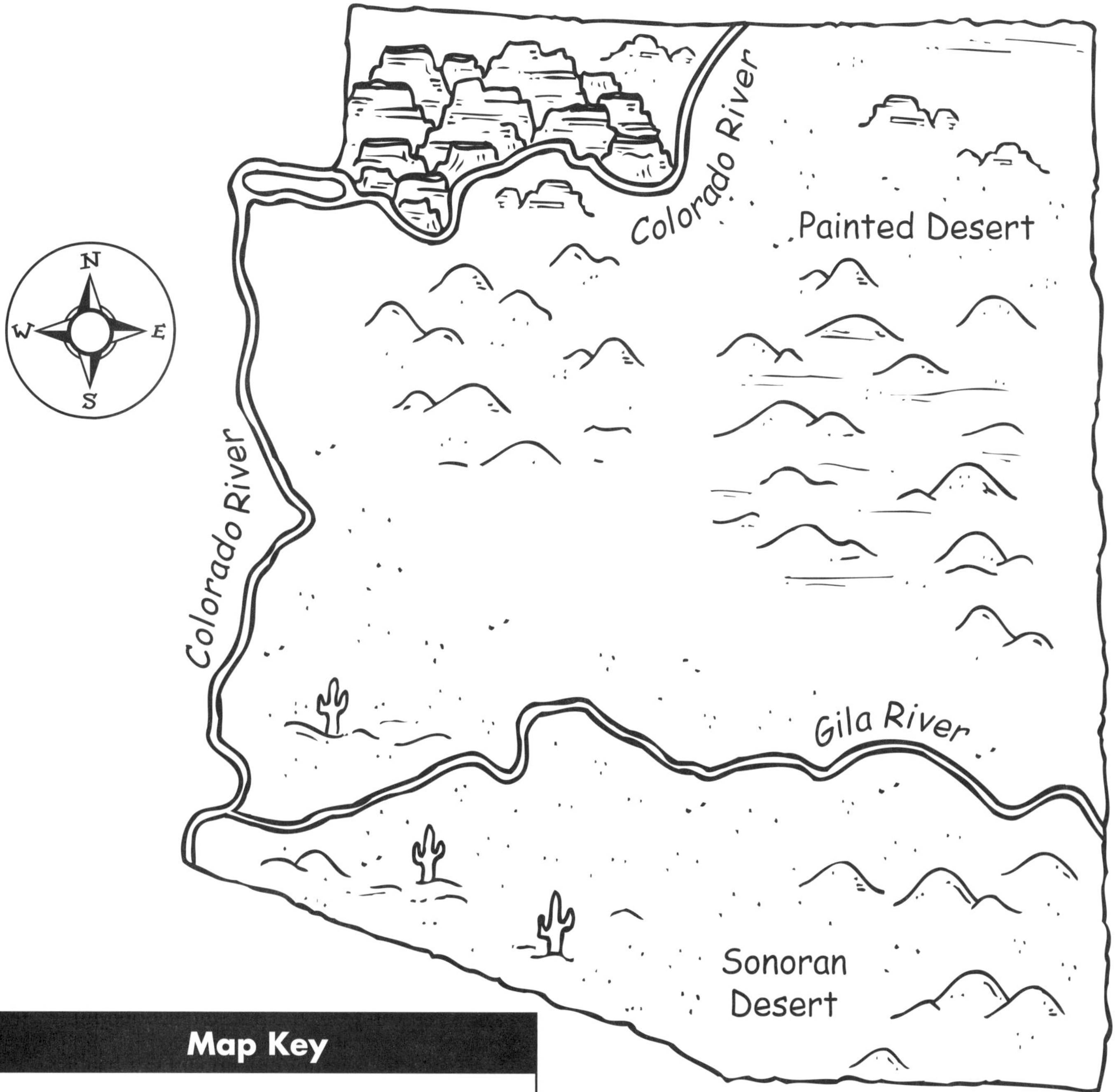

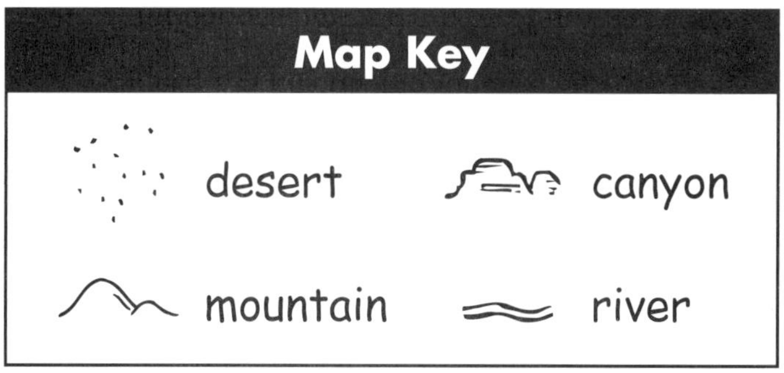

Name ______________________________

Daily Geography

A Land and Water Map of Arizona

WEEK 16

Monday

1. The map shows ________.

   Arizona California

2. The map shows land and ________.

   cities water

Tuesday

1. Which symbol stands for desert?  

2. Which symbol stands for canyon?  

Wednesday

1. Which desert is in the south?

   Painted Desert Sonoran Desert

2. The Grand Canyon is in the ________.

   north south

Name ______________________________

Daily Geography

A Land and Water Map of Arizona

WEEK 16

Thursday

1. The ________ River runs through the Grand Canyon.

   Colorado   Gila

2. The ________ is near the Sonoran Desert.

   Colorado River   Gila River

Friday

1. Canyons, deserts, and mountains are ________.

   land   water

2. Rivers are ________.

   land   water

Challenge

1. Color the Grand Canyon red, yellow, and brown.
2. Color the Painted Desert and Sonoran Desert yellow.
3. Color the mountains brown.
4. Color the rivers blue.

ANSWER KEY

Monday

1. Big
2. Hawaii

Tuesday

1. 
2. 

Wednesday

1. 
2. mountain

Thursday

1. north
2. 5

Friday

1. volcano
2. Pacific Ocean

Challenge

Students should color the volcanoes black and red, the waterfall dark blue, the rest of the island green, and the Pacific Ocean light blue.

A Land and Water Map of Hawaii

Introducing the Map

In this lesson, the physical features of island, ocean, volcano, and waterfall are highlighted. In order to show all four, the map shows only one island of Hawaii. It is the Big Island of Hawaii.

Show students the map of the United States from Week 10. Talk about how the state of Hawaii is made up of many islands. There are eight main islands. Share with students that the largest island has the same name as the state—Hawaii. It is also called "The Big Island."

Then show students the map of Hawaii. Read the symbols on the map key to identify the physical features. First, define an island. Students should notice that the Pacific Ocean is on all sides of the island.

Then tell students about volcanoes. If available, show students pictures of volcanoes from reference books. Tell students that a volcano is a mountain that has an opening. Sometimes lava, or hot liquid rock, comes out of the opening. Sometimes ashes and gases come out, too. Share with students that The Big Island has two active volcanoes. There is one volcano called Kilauea (Kil-a-way-ah) that is always erupting, or sending out lava, ashes, and gases. Have students find the two volcanoes on the island.

Tell students that Hawaii is famous for volcanoes, but it is also famous for its waterfalls. Define *waterfall* for students. Have them find the symbol for it on the map key and then locate it on the map.

In this lesson, students are introduced to two new physical features—volcano and waterfall—as well as reviewing island and ocean from previous lessons.

Introducing Vocabulary

island

An island is land with water all around it.

ocean

An ocean is a large body of water.
Earth has five oceans.

volcano

A volcano is a mountain that has an opening.
Lava, gases, and ashes spill out of the opening.

waterfall

A waterfall is a stream of water falling from a high place.

Name

WEEK 17

A Land and Water Map of Hawaii

This is one island in Hawaii. The island has volcanoes. A volcano is a mountain. It has an opening. Lava, ashes, and gases spill out. The island has waterfalls. A waterfall is a stream of water. The water falls from a high place.

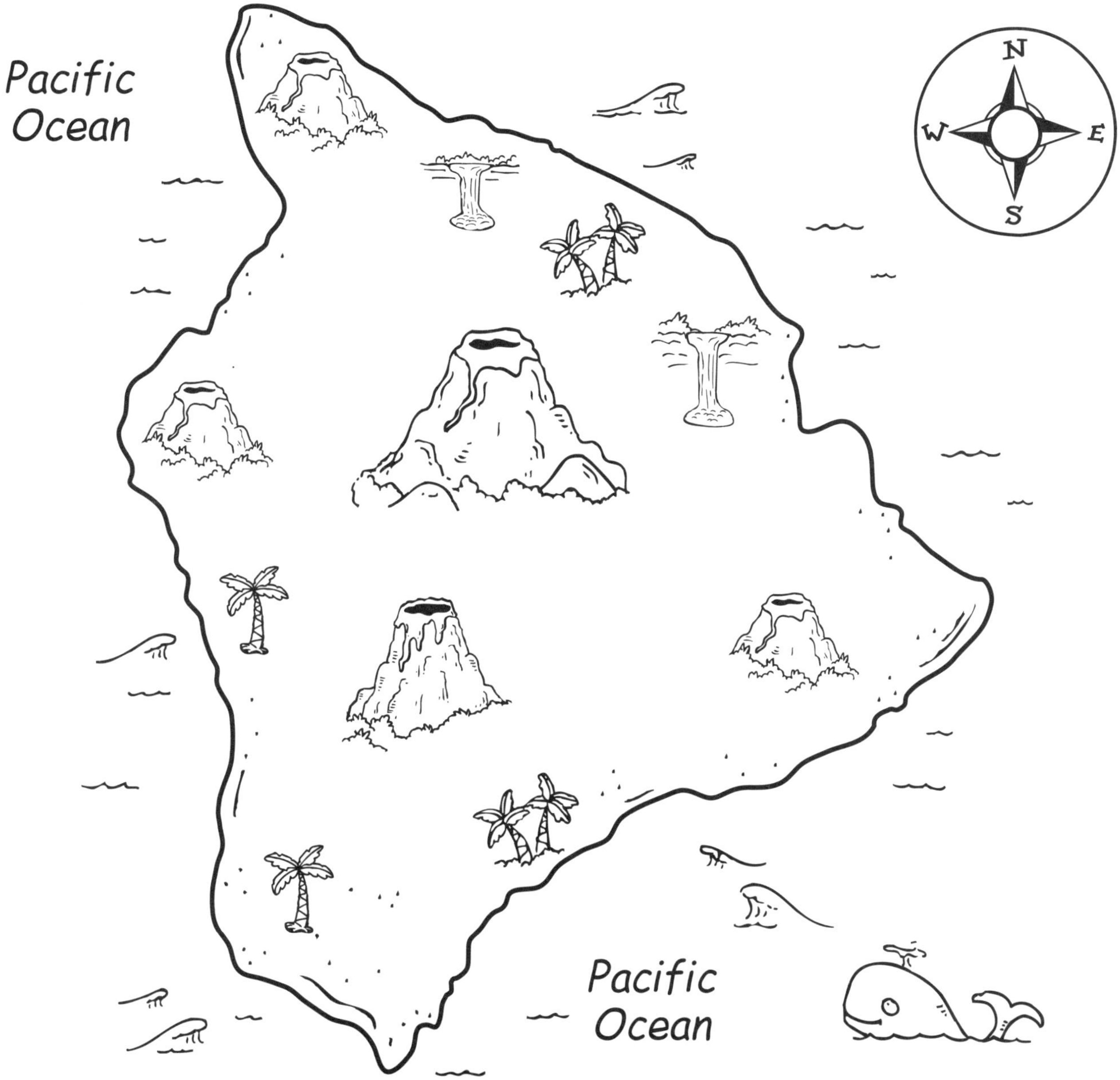

Map Key

volcano — ocean — waterfall

Name ______________________________

Daily Geography

WEEK 17

A Land and Water Map of Hawaii

Monday

1. The map shows the ________ Island.

   Big Little

2. The map shows one island in ________.

   Hawaii California

Tuesday

1. Which symbol stands for ocean?  

2. Which symbol stands for waterfall? 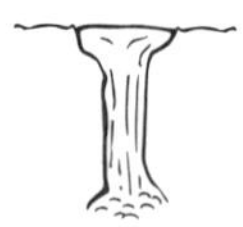 

Wednesday

1. Which symbol stands for volcano?  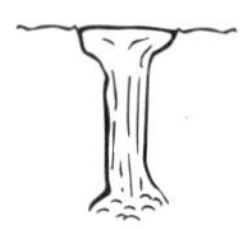

2. A volcano is a kind of ________.

   mountain river

Name ____________________

Daily Geography

WEEK 17

A Land and Water Map of Hawaii

Thursday

1. There are waterfalls in the ________.

   north   south

2. There are ________ volcanoes on the island.

   3   5

Friday

1. Lava spills out of a ________.

   volcano   waterfall

2. Which ocean borders the island of Hawaii?

   ____

Challenge

1. Color the volcanoes black and red.
2. Color the waterfalls dark blue.
3. Color the rest of the island green.
4. Color the Pacific Ocean light blue.

ANSWER KEY

Monday
1. Oregon
2. water

Tuesday
1. 
2. 

Wednesday
1. 
2. 4

Thursday
1. Columbia River
2. Pacific Ocean

Friday
1. Crater Lake
2. half

Challenge
Students should color the mountains brown, the forests green, the lakes dark blue, and the rivers light blue.

A Land and Water Map of Oregon

Introducing the Map

Share with students that some maps show cities. Other maps show things like mountains and rivers. Show students the map of Oregon. Tell them that this state map shows the kinds of land and water Oregon has. Read the caption at the top of the page for students. Then have students look at the map key to see the symbol for each feature.

Oregon is famous for its forests and mountains. There are four mountain ranges shown in Oregon. They are the Cascade Range, the Coast Range, the Klamath Mountains, and the Wallowa Mountains. Tell students that people come to hike, ski, and climb the mountains in Oregon. You may want to share with students that the highest peak in Oregon is Mount Hood in the Cascade Mountains. It rises to 11,239 feet (3,426 m) and is snow-covered much of the year.

Share with students that forests cover nearly half of Oregon. Tell students that the term *forest* is another word for woods. The state has eleven national forests that have beautiful evergreen trees. Oregon's Douglas fir trees can reach heights of 250 feet (76 m). Most Christmas trees that families buy are from Oregon.

Oregon has three important rivers. Name the rivers for them. Help students notice that the Columbia and Snake Rivers border the state. The Willamette River flows into the Columbia River. Talk about the lakes that are labeled on the map. Crater Lake is the deepest lake in the United States. Crater Lake was made from a volcano. Harney and Malheur Lakes are two very large lakes. Tell students that Oregon also borders the Pacific Ocean. When people talk about where Oregon is located, they often say it is in the Pacific Northwest.

In this lesson, students were introduced to five physical features—forests, lakes, mountains, ocean, and rivers.

Introducing Vocabulary

border
A border is a line between two places.
Maps show borders between states or countries.

forest
A forest is a large area covered with many trees.

lake
A lake is a body of water with land all around it.

mountain
A mountain is land that rises very high above the land around it.
It is higher than a hill.

ocean
An ocean is a large body of water. Earth has five oceans.

river
A river is a large stream of water that flows across the land.

Name

A Land and Water Map of Oregon

Half of Oregon is covered in forests. Oregon has large mountains. It has long rivers and deep lakes.

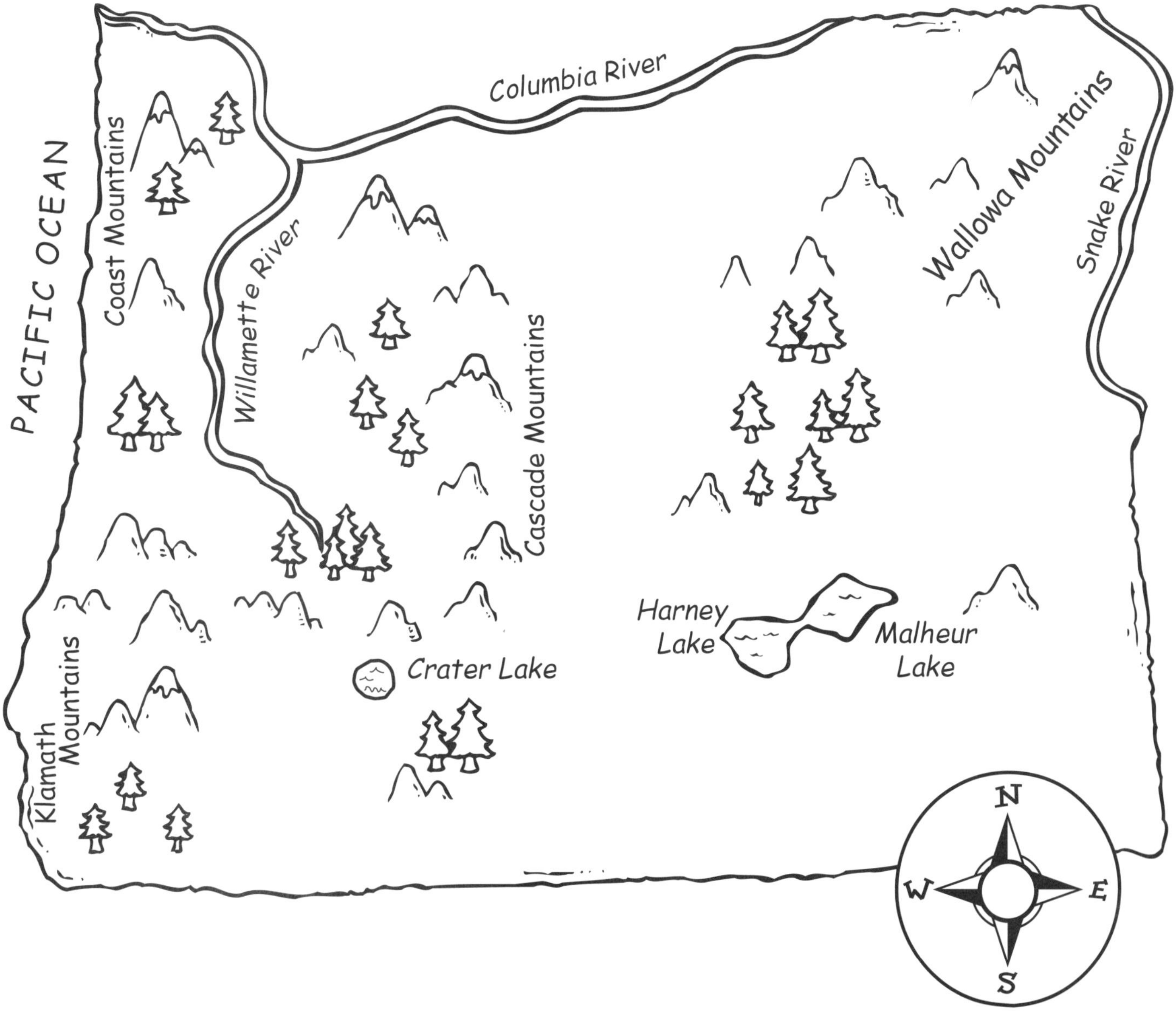

Map Key

forest lake mountain river

Name ______________________________

Daily Geography

WEEK 18

A Land and Water Map of Oregon

Monday

1. The map shows ________.

   Hawaii　　　　Oregon

2. The map shows land and ________.

   cities　　　　water

Tuesday

1. Which symbol stands for forest?  

2. Which symbol stands for lake?  

Wednesday

1. Which symbol stands for mountain?  

2. How many mountains are named on the map?

   2　　　　3　　　　4

Name ____________________

Daily Geography

A Land and Water Map of Oregon

WEEK 18

Thursday

1. Which river borders Oregon on the north?

   Willamette River   Columbia River

2. Which ocean borders Oregon on the west?

   Pacific Ocean   Atlantic Ocean

Friday

1. Which lake is in the Cascade Mountains?

   Crater Lake   Harney Lake

2. How much of Oregon is covered in forests?

   all   half

Challenge

1. Color the mountains brown.
2. Color the forests green.
3. Color the lakes dark blue.
4. Color the rivers light blue.

WEEK 19

Daily Geography

ANSWER KEY

Monday
1. farm
2. countryside

Tuesday
1. barn
2. tractor

Wednesday
1. cows
2. on Rural Route 1

Thursday
1. County Home Road
2. 3

Friday
1. rural area
2. land

Challenge
1. Answers will vary, but students should circle "on a farm" or "in a city."
2. Answers will vary, but students should finish the sentence with their favorite part of the farm.

A Farm Map

Introducing the Map

Share with students that there are different kinds of communities. Most people today live in large cities. But long ago, most of the people lived on small farms or in very small communities. The farm families raised their own cows, chickens, and pigs. They grew their own corn, wheat, fruits, and garden vegetables. Most farm families made enough food for themselves.

Today, there are still farms throughout the United States. But now, each farmer in the United States can make enough food to feed more than 80 people. Tell students that farms are located in rural areas. Rural areas are in the countryside, where there is a lot of land and few people.

Show students the map of a farm. Read the title and caption for students. Help students notice the setting of the farm. Talk about how this farm is in a rural area. It is located outside of town where there is more open space and fewer people. Tell students that the farm is on Rural Route 1, which is the address for the farm. Point out the town in the distance. Talk about the road that leads to the town of Springville. This is called a county road. It used to be called a "farm to market" road. Farmers took their products to nearby towns to sell. This is still done, but now large trucks carry the farm products to towns and cities.

Discuss the things they see on the farm. Ask students if they would like to live in this rural area. Talk about the advantages and disadvantages of living on a farm that is in a rural area. Possible advantages might be that there is more open space to play in. They could raise animals and crops. There would be less traffic. Disadvantages might be that they would live farther away from their friends. They would have to drive into town to get things they want.

This lesson will help students to understand one kind of region. It will also help students to understand the vocabulary associated with a rural area. Review vocabulary throughout the week to check for understanding.

Introducing Vocabulary

countryside
Countryside is land away from cities and towns.

farm
A farm is an area of land.
It is used to grow plants and raise animals.

rural area
A rural area is where farms are.
It is in the countryside.

rural route
A rural route is a farm road.

Name

A Farm Map

A farm is in a rural area. It is in the countryside. There is a lot of land.

My favorite part of the farm is the ______________________.

Name ______________________________

Daily Geography

WEEK 19

A Farm Map

Monday

1. The map shows a ________.

   farm   park

2. The farm is in the ________.

   countryside   town

Tuesday

1. The farm has a house and a ________.

   barn   store

2. The farmer uses a truck and a ________.

   bus   tractor

Wednesday

1. The farmer raises ________.

   cows   pigs

2. The farm is ________.

   on Rural Route 1   in Springville

Name ______________________________

Daily Geography

WEEK 19

A Farm Map

Thursday

1. Which road goes into town?

   Rural Route 1   County Home Road

2. Springville is ________ miles north of the farm.

   1   2   3

Friday

1. The farm is in a ________.

   rural area   town

2. A rural area has a lot of ________.

   land   people

Challenge

1. Where would you like to live?

   on a farm   in a city

2. What is your favorite part of the farm?
   Finish the sentence on the map.

A Town Map

Introducing the Map

Share with students that there are different kinds of communities. There are rural areas where there is a lot of land, but only a few people live there. Farms are in rural areas or in the countryside. Another kind of community is called a town. A town has neighborhoods with people and buildings in it. A town is not as big as a city.

Show students the map of Youngtown. Read the caption at the top of the map to students. Discuss how a town is a place where people live and work. A town is made up of neighborhoods. On the streets are houses and other buildings. Name the buildings in Youngtown. Point out the fire station. Ask students on which street the fire station is located. The fire station, hospital, and bank are all on Oak Street. Have students find other buildings on the map.

Talk about how there are usually one or more highways located on the edge of a town. In Youngtown, there is Highway 1. That highway may lead to another town or to a bigger city.

In this lesson, students are introduced to another area, or region, called a town. Students should begin to understand that a town is larger than a farm in a rural area, but is smaller than a city.

Review vocabulary with students throughout the week to check for understanding.

Introducing Vocabulary

city
A city is a very large or important town.

community
A community is a group of people who live together in the same area.

neighborhood
A neighborhood is a small area in a city where people live.

street
A street is a road in a town or city.
Most streets have buildings on both sides.

town
A town is a place where people live and work.
A town is smaller than a city.

WEEK 20

Daily Geography

ANSWER KEY

Monday
1. town
2. Youngtown

Tuesday
1. houses
2. park

Wednesday
1. work
2. post office

Thursday
1. fire station
2. bank

Friday
1. Highway 1
2. town

Challenge
Answers will vary. Encourage students to color one house yellow, the park green, and one of the other seven areas of the town red.

Name

A Town Map

This map shows Youngtown. People live, work, and play there.

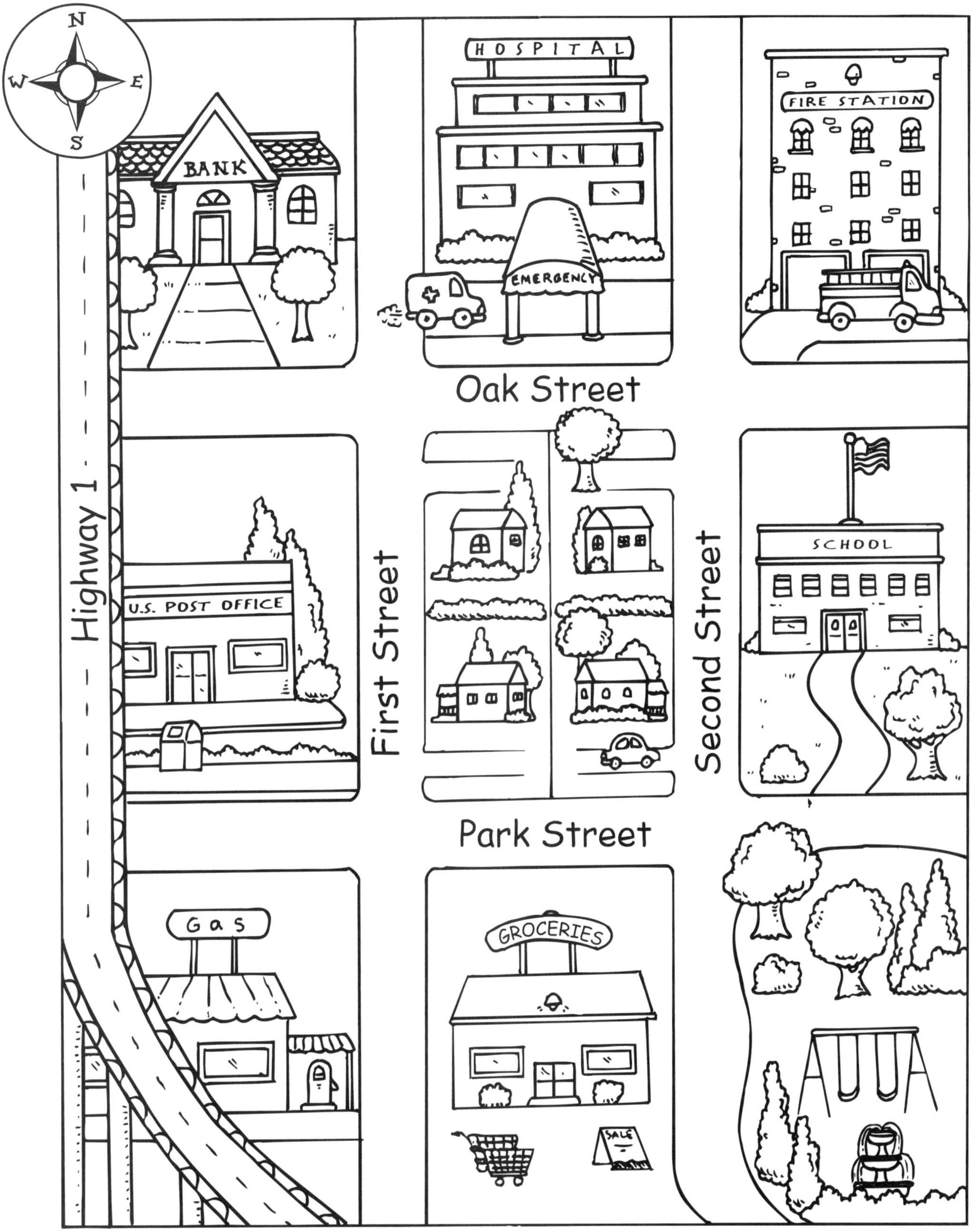

Name ______________________________

Daily Geography

WEEK 20

A Town Map

Monday

1. The map shows a ________.

   farm town

2. The name of the town is ________.

   Oak Town Youngtown

Tuesday

1. Where do people live?

   houses school

2. Where do children play?

   bank park

Wednesday

1. People ________ at the gas station.

   work play

2. What is on Park Street?

   hospital post office

Name ____________________

Daily Geography

WEEK 20

A Town Map

Thursday

1. What is on Oak Street?

   fire station　　　　gas station

2. What is not on Second Street?

   bank　　　　park

Friday

1. Which road is west of Youngtown?

   Highway 1　　　　Second Street

2. Which one has more people?

   farm　　　　town

Challenge

1. Color one place to live in Youngtown yellow.
2. Color one place to play in Youngtown green.
3. Color one place to work in Youngtown red.

WEEK 21

Daily Geography

A City Map

Introducing the Map

Share with students that there are different kinds of communities. In Weeks 19 and 20, a rural area and a town were highlighted. Another kind of community is a city. Tell students that a city is a community where thousands, or even millions, of people live and work. A city is a large, busy, and crowded place.

Show students the map of a city. Discuss with students how many large cities have a central section, called the downtown area. Point out the different buildings in the downtown area. There is a bank, a department store, a museum, an outdoor café, and apartment buildings. Be sure to explain what is found in each of these buildings. To save space in a crowded city, people build their buildings tall and narrow. They are called skyscrapers.

There is also a city park where people can bike, walk, or jog. Talk about how many people in a city use public transportation such as buses, subways, and trains to get around the city.

In this lesson, students should begin to understand the concept of a big city and how busy and crowded it can be. Discuss the advantages and disadvantages of living in a big city. People find it exciting to live where there are tall skyscrapers, museums, and busy streets. Others find living in a city more difficult because it is so crowded and noisy.

Review vocabulary throughout the week to check for understanding.

Introducing Vocabulary

city
A city is a very large or important town.

community
A community is a group of people who live together in the same area.

downtown
Downtown is a city's main business area.

skyscraper
A skyscraper is a very tall building.

ANSWER KEY

Monday
1. big city
2. Central City

Tuesday
1. tall
2. close to

Wednesday
1. bus
2. Garden Apartments

Thursday
1. City Museum
2. Park Avenue

Friday
1. city
2. skyscrapers

Challenge
1. Answers will vary. Students should color a favorite place on the map.
2. Students should circle yes or no to the question on the map.

Optional: Have students tell you why they would or would not like to live in Central City.

A City Map

This city is a very large town. It is a busy and crowded place. It has many tall buildings called skyscrapers.

Central City

Would you like to live in Central City? yes no

Name ______________________________

Daily Geography

WEEK 21

A City Map

Monday

1. The map shows a ________.

   big city   small town

2. The name of the city is ________.

   Bank City   Central City

Tuesday

1. There are a lot of ________ buildings in a city.

   red   tall

2. The buildings in a city are ________ each other.

   close to   far from

Wednesday

1. There is a car, a truck, and a ________ on the streets.

   bus   train

2. People live in the ________.

   City Museum   Garden Apartments

Name ______________________________

Daily Geography

WEEK 21

A City Map

Thursday

1. What is on First Street?

   City Museum   City Park

2. The bus stop is on ________.

   First Street   Park Avenue

Friday

1. Which one has more people?

   city   farm   town

2. The city has very tall buildings called ________.

   skyscrapers   museums

Challenge

1. Color your favorite place in Central City.
2. Would you like to live in Central City? Circle your answer on the map.

WEEK 22

Daily Geography

ANSWER KEY

Monday
1. Texas
2. state

Tuesday
1. ⊙
2. capital

Wednesday
1. Austin
2. — — —

Thursday
1. Brownsville
2. El Paso

Friday
1. south
2. larger

Challenge
Students should color the city of Austin yellow and the city of Dallas blue. They should trace the state border of Texas in green.

A State Map

Introducing the Map

Talk about the different kinds of communities. There are communities such as rural or farm communities, small towns, and large cities. Tell students that there are many kinds of communities in a state. Define state and discuss how the United States is made up of 50 states.

Show students the state map of Texas. Read the information about Texas to students. Have students look at the map key. Talk about how this map key shows the capital, cities, and the border of Texas. Explain that the capital of a state is a special city. It is where the leaders of the state work. On the map, a star shows where the capital is located. Have students find the capital of Texas. They should find Austin on the map. Read the names of the other cities on the map. Each city is represented by a dot. Share with students that only a few of the larger cities are on the map. Texas has many more cities and towns. It also has many cattle ranches, which are large farms, throughout the state.

Talk about the dotted line that surrounds the state. Tell students that this is the border line for Texas. Then have students look at the small map of the United States with Texas highlighted. Help students notice where Texas is located and note that it is one of the largest states in size. You may wish to refer back to Week 10 "Picturing the United States" to show students a larger map of the U.S. and the location of Texas on that map as well. Also, review the simple compass rose to help students with the four main directions on a map.

In this lesson, students should begin to understand what a state is. It is an area that contains farms or rural areas, towns, and cities. It has a special city called the capital. Students should also begin to understand that the United States is made up of 50 states and that there are borders for each state. Review with students the name of their town or city and their state to help them make the connection.

Introducing Vocabulary

border
A border is a line between two places. Maps show borders between states or countries.

capital
A capital is a special city. It is where the leaders of the state work.

city
A city is a very large or important town.

direction
A direction tells where something is found. The four main directions are north, south, east, and west.

map key
A map key shows the symbols on a map. It tells what each symbol stands for.

state
A state is part of a country. There are 50 states in the United States.

A State Map

This map shows Texas. Texas is a large state.
It is in the United States.

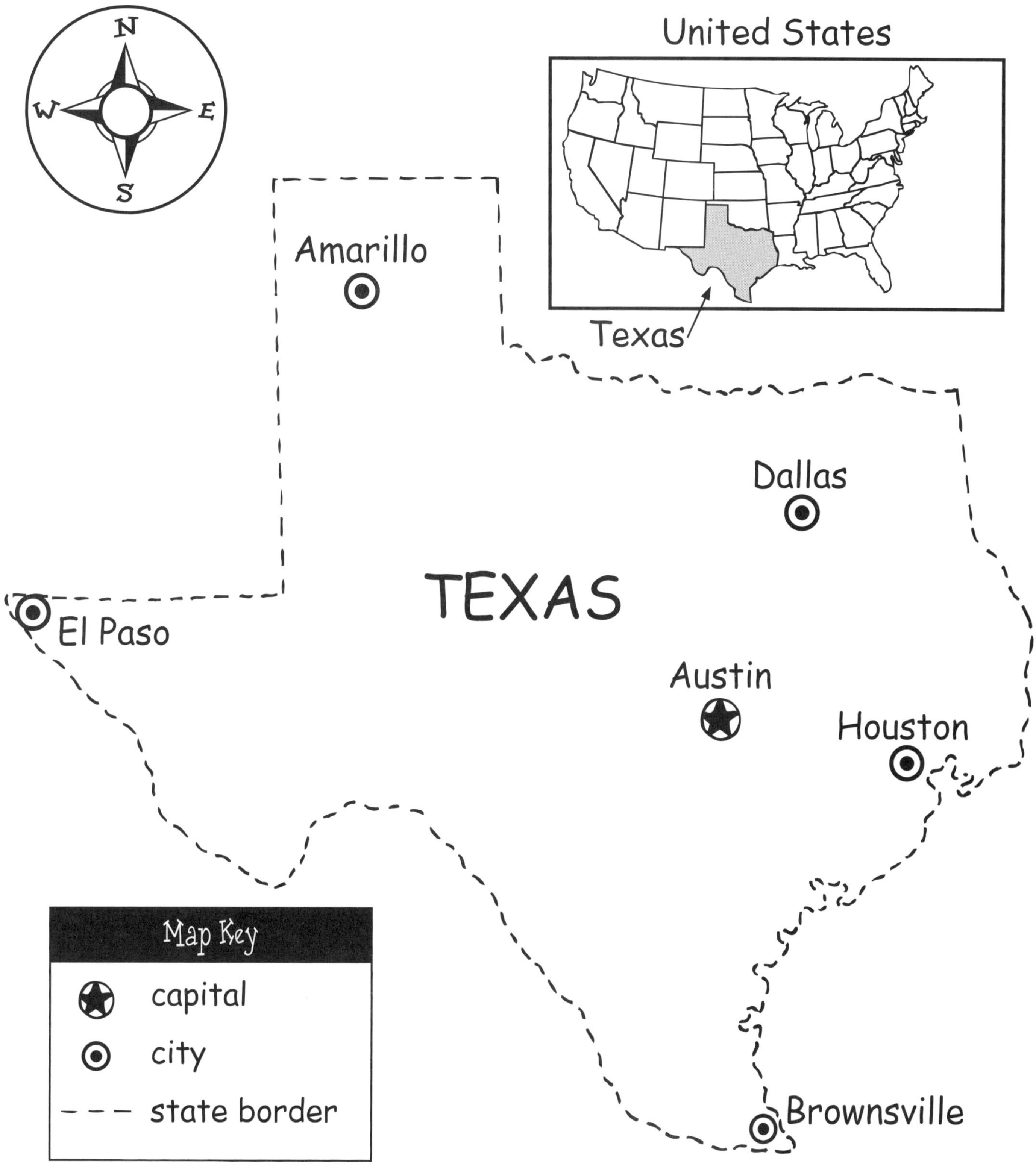

Name ______________________________

A State Map

Monday

1. The map shows ________.

   California   Texas

2. Texas is a ________.

   city   state

Tuesday

1. Which symbol stands for a city?    

2. A  stands for a ________.

   capital   city

Wednesday

1. The capital of Texas is ________.

   Austin   Dallas

2. What shows the border around Texas?

      – – – –

Name ______________________________

Daily Geography

WEEK 22

A State Map

Thursday

1. Which city is in the south?

   Amarillo Brownsville

2. Which city is west of Austin?

   El Paso Houston

Friday

1. Texas is in the ________ part of the United States.

   north south

2. Texas is one of the ________ states.

   larger smaller

Challenge

1. Color the capital yellow.
2. Color the city of Dallas blue.
3. Trace the border of Texas in green.

WEEK 23

Daily Geography

ANSWER KEY

Monday
1. Zoo
2. 6

Tuesday
1. 
2. 

Wednesday
1. 
2. food

Thursday
1. bears
2. lions

Friday
1. elephants
2. east and west

Challenge
1. Students should color the animals on the map.
2. Answers will vary. Students should write the name of their favorite animal at the bottom of the page.

A Zoo Map

Introducing the Map

Ask students to name their favorite zoo animal. Students might say animals such as elephants, lions, monkeys, or giraffes. Ask students how many of them have visited a zoo. Tell students that zoos are very popular places for families to visit. People love to look at animals that are from all over the world. If there is a zoo in your community, talk about what makes your zoo so popular.

Discuss with students that there are more than 10,000 zoos around the world. Share with students that many large cities have a zoo, but small towns can have one, too. Large zoos can have a huge variety of animals. The Bronx Zoo in New York has more than 11,000 animals. The San Diego Zoo in California has more than 12,000 animals. Mammals such as lions, elephants, and monkeys are common in zoos. There are also reptiles like alligators and snakes in zoos. Zoos display many kinds of birds, and even insects can be in zoos.

Show students the map of the zoo. Have students look at the different areas of the zoo. Look at the map key and have students look at the symbols for each of the animals. Read the names of the animals for students. Have students find the symbol for a bear. Then ask students to look at the map to find where the bear is found at the zoo. Have students use the map key to find other animals. Ask students what the symbol for food is. They should recognize that a hot dog stands for food. Have students locate the Snack Shack in the middle of the zoo. Review the compass rose directions with students as well.

In this lesson, students are introduced to the idea of zoos as cultural landmarks. Zoos are important places. They provide family fun, excitement, educational programs, and a peaceful setting to enjoy nature.

Introducing Vocabulary

direction
A direction tells where something is found.
The four main directions are north, south, east, and west.

landmark
A landmark is an important place or building.
A zoo is a landmark.

map key
A map key shows the symbols on a map.
It tells what each symbol stands for.

symbol
A symbol is a drawing that stands for something real.

zoo
A zoo is a place where people come to see wild animals.

Name

A Zoo Map

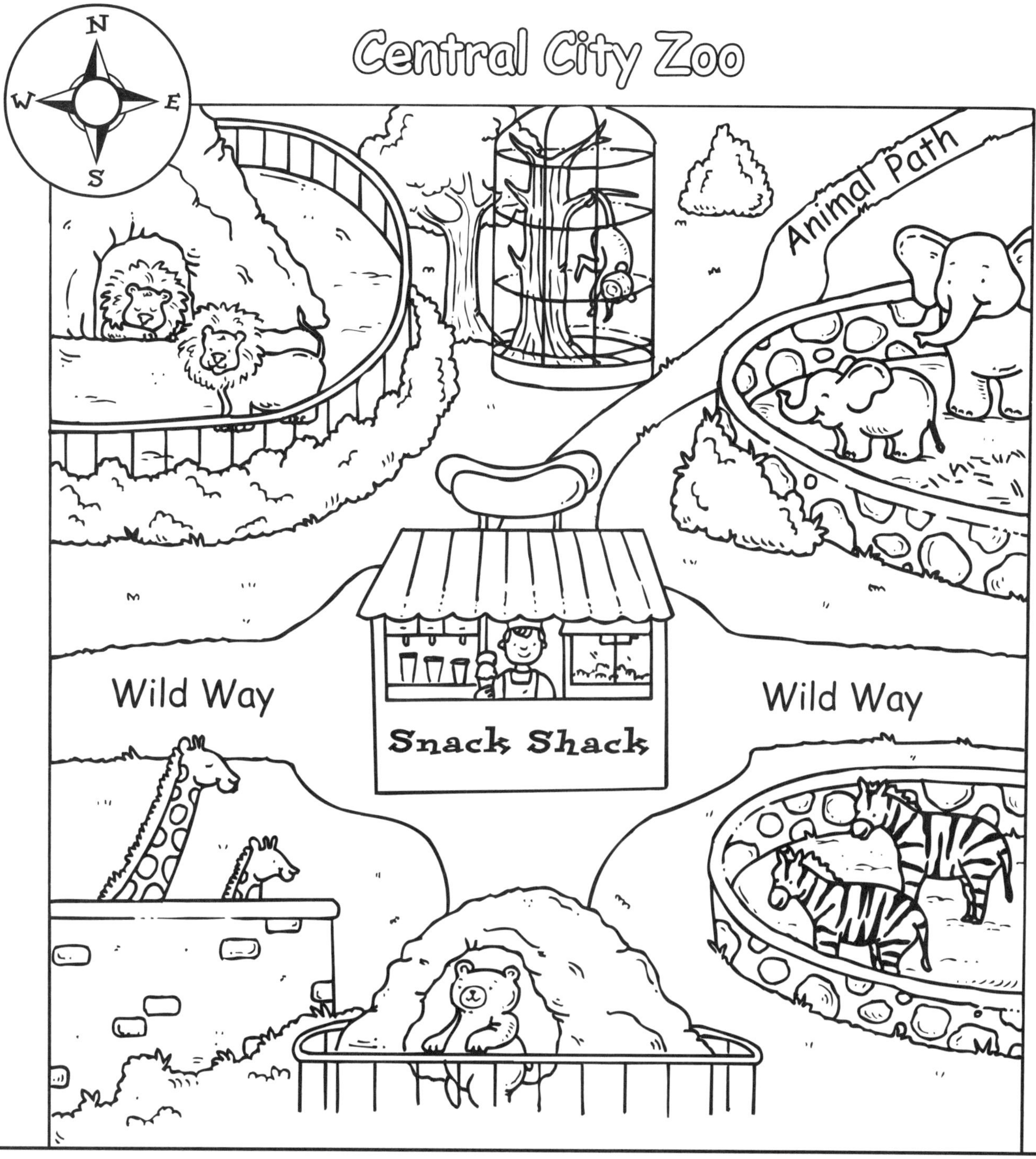

Map Key

Bears	Giraffes	Zebras	Elephants
Lions	Food	Monkeys	

Which zoo animal is your favorite? ____________________

Name ____________________

Daily Geography

WEEK 23

A Zoo Map

Monday

1. The map shows Central City ________.

   Park　　　　　　　　　Zoo

2. How many kinds of animals are on the map key?

   ____

Tuesday

1. Which symbol stands for lions?  

2. Which symbol stands for elephants?  

Wednesday

1. Which symbol stands for zebras?  

2.  stands for ________.

   animals　　　　　　　　　food

Name ______________________________

Daily Geography

WEEK 23

A Zoo Map

Thursday

1. What is south of the Snack Shack?

   bears　　　　monkeys

2. What is north and west of the Snack Shack?

   lions　　　　zebras

Friday

1. What is east of the Animal Path?

   elephants　　　　lions

2. Wild Way runs ________.

   east and west　　　　north and south

Challenge

1. Color the zoo animals at Central City Zoo.
2. Which zoo animal is your favorite?
   Write its name on the map.

Daily Geography

ANSWER KEY

Monday
1. fun park
2. rides

Tuesday
1. 6
2. Ferris wheel

Wednesday
1. Snack Shack
2. Merry-Go-Round

Thursday
1. Log Ride
2. restrooms

Friday
1. south
2. Ferris wheel

Challenge
1. Answers will vary. Students should color one of the six rides.
2. Answers will vary. Students should write the name of one of the rides on the map.

A Fun Park Map

Introducing the Map

Ask students to name a special place they would like to go for a vacation. Many students will probably say Disneyland or Disney World. That is because amusement parks, or fun parks, have become important landmarks in American culture. Ask students to name some fun things to do at an amusement park.

Share with students that fun parks have been around for over 400 years. The first fun parks were called "Pleasure Gardens." The gardens were filled with games, music, and the first fun rides. The roller coaster and the Ferris wheel were two of the first rides to be invented. After that, more and more rides were invented.

Amusement parks are all over the country now. When families think about a fun family vacation, they often think of going to fun parks. Share with students that when people are asked to name a famous place in the United States, many people say "Disneyland." They say Disneyland more often than the Statue of Liberty or the White House. That's how popular fun parks are.

Show students the map of a fun park. Share with students that when they enter a fun park, they are given a map. This map helps them find their way around the park. That way, they can plan which rides to go on and not waste a lot of time just walking around. Read and discuss the different rides at the park. Point out the entrance at the south end of the park and the exit at the north end of the park. Also, discuss where students can go to buy gifts, to eat, and where to use the restrooms.

In this lesson, students are introduced to the cultural landmark of an amusement park. Students are not expected to define amusement park. It has been included for your reference. You may choose to introduce the term, which may be familiar to many students. Students will begin to understand that fun parks have maps to follow. These maps help them find places more easily. Encourage students to read the maps at the parks that they visit from now on.

Introducing Vocabulary

amusement park (not included in the glossary)
An amusement park is a fun place.
It has rides, food, and shops.

enter
To enter is to go into a place.

exit
The exit is the way out of a place.

landmark
A landmark is an important place or building.
A zoo is a landmark.

Name

A Fun Park Map

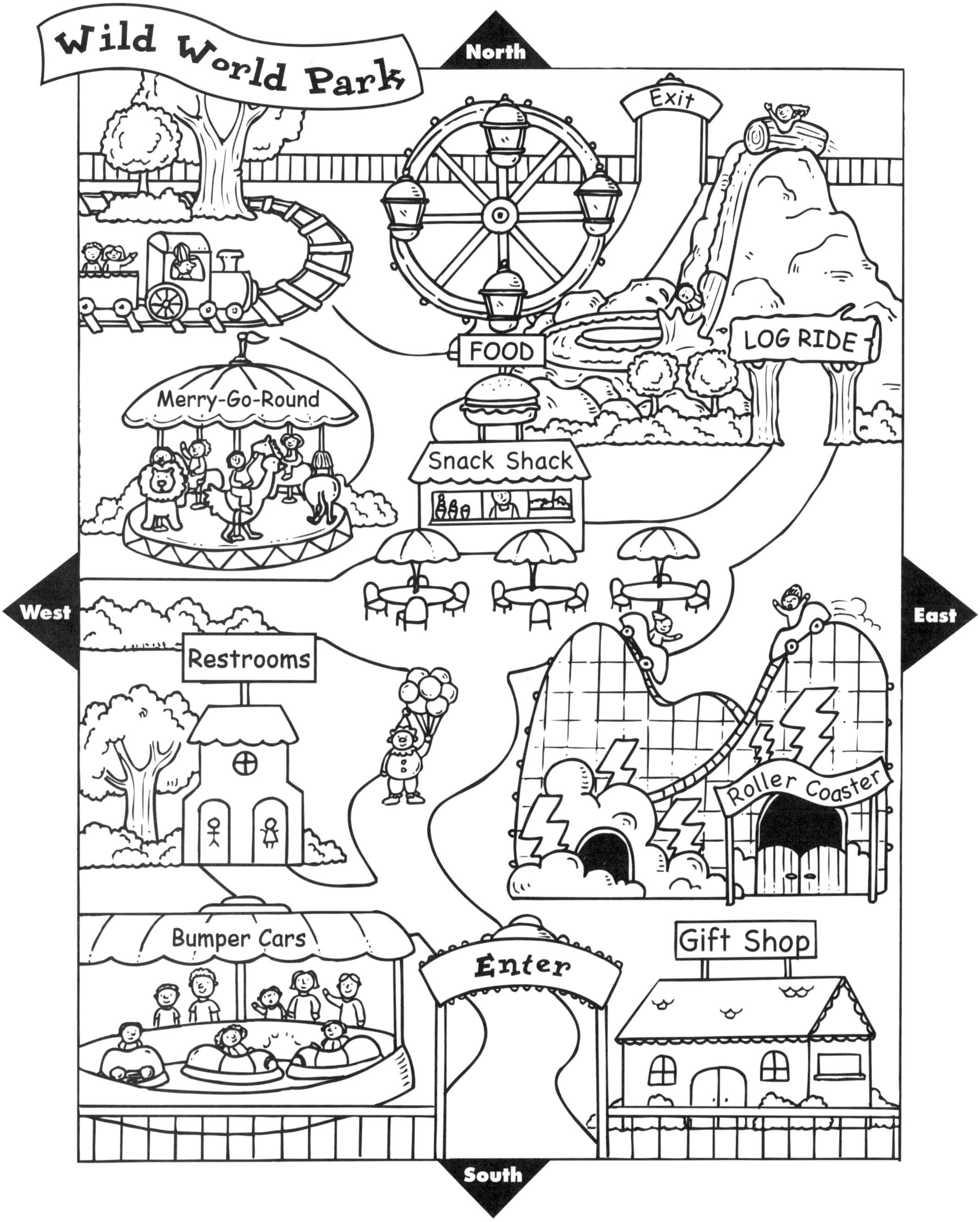

I like the ______________________________ the best.

Name ______________________________

Daily Geography

WEEK 24

A Fun Park Map

Monday

1. The map shows a ________.

   fun park   petting zoo

2. What is at Wild World Park?

   animals   rides

Tuesday

1. How many rides are there?

   3   6

2. One of the rides is a ________.

   Ferris wheel   Rocket

Wednesday

1. Where can you eat?

   Log Ride   Snack Shack

2. What is next to the Snack Shack?

   Merry-Go-Round   Train

Name ______________________________

Daily Geography

WEEK 24

A Fun Park Map

Thursday

1. Which ride gets you wet?

   Log Ride   Train Ride

2. The clown is next to the ________.

   gift shop   restrooms

Friday

1. You enter the park at the ________ end.

   north   south

2. What is near the exit?

   Bumper Cars   Ferris wheel

Challenge

1. Color your favorite ride at the fun park.
2. Write which ride you like best on the map.

WEEK 25

Daily Geography

ANSWER KEY

Monday

1. weather map
2. 5

Tuesday

1. 
2. 

Wednesday

1. 
2. rain

Thursday

1. snowy
2. sunny

Friday

1. clouds
2. winter

Challenge

1. Answers will vary. Students should color one of the five states that shows their favorite kind of weather.
2. Answers will vary. Students should write the name of their favorite state and the kind of weather it has in the blanks.

A Weather Map

Introducing the Map

Ask students to describe the weather outside. Depending on your area, students may use words like sunny, rainy, or stormy. Introduce the term weather. Explain to students that weather is what the air is like at a certain time and place. Tell students that there are many kinds of weather. The weather may be warm and sunny in one place and cold and raining in another.

Show students the weather map of five North-Central states in the United States. Read the caption at the top of the page for students. Name the states for the students as well. Talk about where they would see a weather map. Newspapers have weather maps. Weather maps are also shown on television. You may have a weather map in your classroom. Talk about how it is important for people to know about the weather. They can plan what to wear and which activities to do according to the weather outside.

Look at the weather symbols used on the map key. Have students find the symbol for sunny. Then have students look at the map to find the state that is sunny. Students should find that Iowa is having a sunny day.

Talk about which states are having good weather and which ones are having stormy weather. Discuss how seasons of the year have certain kinds of weather. Help students think about which season of the year would produce these kinds of weather conditions. Students should conclude that since it is snowing in Minnesota and North Dakota, it is probably winter.

In this lesson, students are introduced to another kind of map—the weather map. They also practice using a map key and compass rose.

Introducing Vocabulary

map key
A map key shows the symbols on a map.
It tells what each symbol stands for.

season
A season is one of the four parts of the year.
The seasons are fall, winter, spring, and summer.

state
A state is part of a country.
There are 50 states in the United States.

weather
Weather is what the air is like at a certain place and time.
Warm and sunny is a kind of weather.

A Weather Map

This map shows five states. It shows the weather in each state. The weather is what the air outside is like.

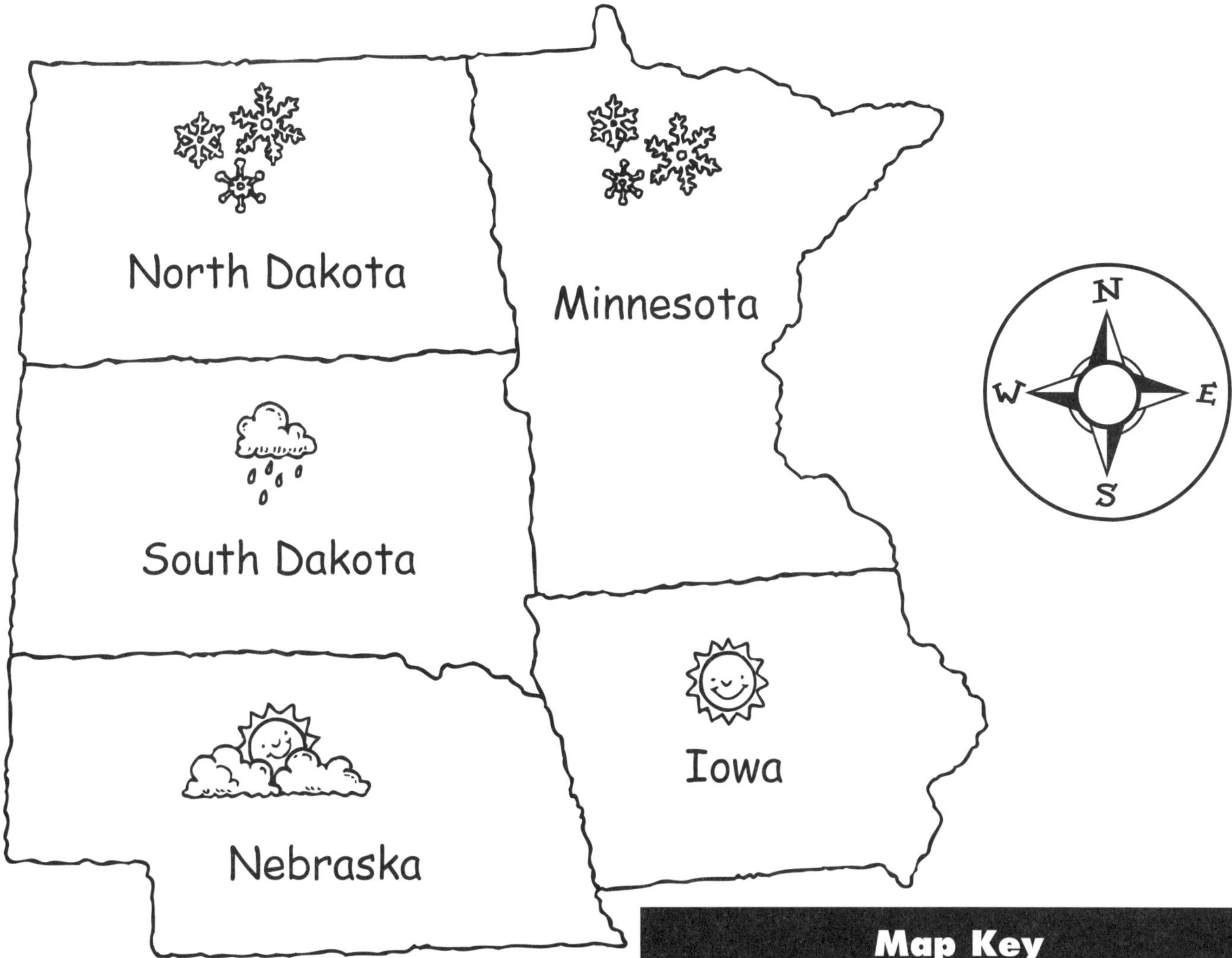

I like the state of ______________________________.

The weather is ______________________________.

Name ______________________________

Daily Geography

WEEK 25

A Weather Map

Monday

1. What kind of map is it?

   land and water map　　　　weather map

2. The weather map shows ________ states.

   5　　　　6

Tuesday

1. Which symbol stands for sunny?

2. Which symbol stands for partly cloudy?

Wednesday

1. Which symbol stands for snow?

2. South Dakota is having ________.

   rain　　　　snow

Name ____________________

Daily Geography

WEEK 25

A Weather Map

Thursday

1. What is the weather in North Dakota?

   rainy snowy

2. What is the weather in Iowa?

   partly cloudy sunny

Friday

1. Nebraska and South Dakota have ________.

   clouds rain

2. Which season of the year is it?

   summer winter

Challenge

1. Color one state that has your favorite kind of weather.
2. Finish the sentences on the map.

WEEK 26

Daily Geography

ANSWER KEY

Monday
1. desert
2. hot

Tuesday
1. snake
2. cactus

Wednesday
1. sand
2. dry

Thursday
1. mountains
2. cool

Friday
1. a home
2. animals, plants, and people

Challenge
Provide pictures of the desert animals for students. Help students choose an animal to draw, or designate one you would like them to add to the desert map.

A Desert Habitat

Introducing the Map

Introduce the term habitat. Discuss different kinds of habitats such as forests, grasslands, and oceans. Tell students there is another kind of habitat called the desert. For the purposes of this lesson, a hot desert in the U.S. will be the focus.

Show students the map of a desert habitat. Tell students that this desert has sandy and rocky soil. It gets less than 10 inches (25 cm) of rain each year. It is very hot in the daytime, especially during the summer. Temperatures can reach 100 degrees or more. Tell students that even though it is hot and dry, animals, plants, and people live in this desert.

Discuss how it is not easy for animals and plants to live in the desert. Talk about how animals and plants have to adapt to the hot sun and the lack of water. For example, some animals get water from the plants and seeds they eat. Meat-eaters get water from the animals they eat. Other animals lick the dew that forms at night. Some animals hide during the hot day and hunt at night. Others dig holes under the ground to live. Common desert animals are lizards and snakes.

Plants like the cactus grow far apart. That way, they don't have to fight for water. Some plants' roots spread way out. Other plants have long roots. These roots get water from deep in the soil. Some plants store water for long periods. Other plants only grow when it rains. The desert has beautiful flowers for a short time during the rains.

Tell students that people live in the desert, too. Most people live in the cities of the desert areas of the United States. The Sonoran Desert is in Arizona and California, and parts of Mexico. Many people have moved to this area. Water is a problem. Many people use adobe brick to build their houses. This kind of brick keeps the houses cooler. People use desert plants around their houses. Many do not plant lawns because they need too much water.

Students should get a basic understanding of how people, plants, and animals have learned how to live in the desert. Review vocabulary throughout the week.

Introducing Vocabulary

adobe
Adobe is a brick made of clay.
It is mixed with straw and dried in the sun.

desert
A desert is a dry, sandy, or rocky area of land.

habitat
A habitat is a place where a plant or animal lives.
A habitat gives food, water, and shelter.
A desert is a habitat.

Name

A Desert Habitat

This desert is hot and dry. It has rocky and sandy land. Animals live in the desert. Cactus plants live in the desert. People live in the desert. The desert is their habitat. It is their home.

Name ____________________________________

Daily Geography

WEEK 26

A Desert Habitat

Monday

1. The map shows a ________.

    desert   forest

2. The map shows a ________ desert.

    cold   hot

Tuesday

1. A ________ is an animal on the map.

    snake   cactus

2. A ________ is a plant on the map.

    lizard   cactus

Wednesday

1. A desert has rocks and ________.

    grass   sand

2. The air is hot and ________.

    wet   dry

Name ____________________________

Daily Geography

WEEK 26

A Desert Habitat

Thursday

1. What is in the north part of the desert?

   mountains   rivers

2. Adobe houses help people stay ________.

   cool   warm

Friday

1. A habitat is ________.

   a home   an animal

2. A desert habitat is for ________.

   only plants   animals, plants, and people

Challenge

Here are more desert animals.

coyote	jackrabbit	kangaroo rat
roadrunner	scorpion	tarantula

1. Choose one desert animal from the list.
2. Draw it on the map.

Skill: Population | Essential Element 4: Standard 9

Moving to the City

Introducing the Map

Ask students if they have ever moved. Give one or two students an opportunity to share their experiences of moving. Tell students that forty-two million people in the United States move every year. That is a large number of people that move from place to place.

Ask students why people move. Tell students that people move for many reasons. People move because of their jobs. They find new jobs in different cities. Some people move when they buy or rent a new house or apartment. People move so they can be closer to their families. Some students move out of their homes and go to college or go to work in different towns and cities. Some older people move when they stop working. They move into smaller homes or to warmer places.

Share with students that a lot of people move from smaller towns to larger cities. In larger cities, there usually are more jobs for people. Show students the map of the small town and the larger city. Help students notice the moving van in the small town of Springville. They should see the sign for Springville. Read the population of Springville—5,000 people. Explain that population means the total number of people who live in that town.

Tell students it is moving day for the Brown family. They are moving to a larger city called Parker. Point out Highway 5 to the students. Have students follow the highway from Springville to Parker. Help students read the population of Parker—50,000 people. Mr. and Mrs. Brown have new jobs in Parker. The family is going to live in an apartment. Their children, Tom and Cathy, will go to a new school, and they will meet new friends.

Help the students understand that when the Brown family moves out of Springville, the population will be smaller. The population of Parker will be larger because it is getting more people.

In this lesson, students are introduced to the term population. Students begin to understand that populations of towns and cities change when people move in and out of them.

Introducing Vocabulary

city
A city is a very large or important town.

highway
A highway is a main road.

population
The population is the total number of people who live in a place.

town
A town is a place where people live and work.
A town is smaller than a city.

WEEK 27

Daily Geography

ANSWER KEY

Monday
1. city
2. moving

Tuesday
1. Springville
2. Parker

Wednesday
1. Springville
2. Parker

Thursday
1. 5
2. 5,000

Friday
1. Parker
2. jobs

Challenge
1. Answers will vary, but students should fill in the name of either Parker or Springville at the bottom of the page.
2. Answers will vary, but students should fill in the population of either Parker (50,000) or Springville (5,000).

Name

Moving to the City

The Brown family is moving. Mr. and Mrs. Brown have new jobs. They are leaving Springville. They are moving to Parker.

I would like to live in ______________________________.

The population is ______________________________ people.

Name ________________________________

Daily Geography

WEEK 27

Moving to the City

Monday

1. The map shows a town and a ________.

   city   state

2. The Brown family is ________.

   moving   playing

Tuesday

1. The Brown family is leaving ________.

   Parker   Springville

2. The Brown family is moving to ________.

   Parker   Springville

Wednesday

1. Which one is a small town?

   Parker   Springville

2. Which one is a city?

   Parker   Springville

Name ______________________________

Daily Geography

WEEK 27

Moving to the City

Thursday

1. The moving van will go on Highway ________.

   1 3 5

2. How many people live in Springville?

   5,000 50,000

Friday

1. There are more people in ________.

   Parker Springville

2. Mr. and Mrs. Brown are moving because they have new ________.

   jobs cars

Challenge

Would you like to live in Springville or Parker?

1. Write which place you would like to live on the map.
2. Write its population.

ANSWER KEY

Monday
1. county fair
2. outside

Tuesday
1. farm
2. 6

Wednesday
1. Ferris wheel
2. Any one of the following: hot dogs, ice cream, or pizza

Thursday
1. rugs
2. teddy bear

Friday
1. singing
2. north

Challenge
1. Answers will vary. Students should color their favorite area.
2. Answers will vary. Students should name their favorite area.

A County Fair Map

Introducing the Map

Explain to students that families have special things they do year after year. It may be a family vacation to a cabin, a holiday celebration at Grandma's, or watching the fireworks on the 4th of July. Tell students that those are customs. A custom is a group's special way of doing something.

One custom many communities have is a county fair. Ask students if they have ever gone to a county fair. Talk about what they have seen and done at the fair.

Explain to students that a county fair is held every year. The county fair includes farm animals, exhibits, shows, rides, games, and food. People from the community often enter their handmade goods such as art, crafts, and homegrown fruits and vegetables into a contest. People show farm animals they have raised. The animals are judged and receive ribbons. Carnivals are also part of the county fair. Sometimes there are shows where people perform, too.

Show students the county fair map. Talk about the different areas and what kinds of things are located in each area. Be sure to read the labels on the map. Further explain the arts and crafts area. This is where homemade things are displayed and judged. Ask students to name their favorite area of this county fair.

In this lesson, students are introduced to the custom of a county fair. The custom of county fairs comes from farming traditions. The first county fairs were held to show farm animals. County fairs grew to include showing foods from the garden and homemade clothing and crafts. Carnivals and stage shows were added, along with many other activities. Today, there are 3,200 county fairs held in North America. County fairs have become part of America's cultural heritage.

Introducing Vocabulary

carnival
A carnival is a fair with rides and games.

county fair
A county fair is an outdoor show.
A county fair shows animals and has fun things to do.

custom
A custom is a special way that people do things.
Going to a county fair every year is a custom.

A County Fair Map

A county fair is an outdoor show. People show their animals. They show things they made. There are games, rides, and food.

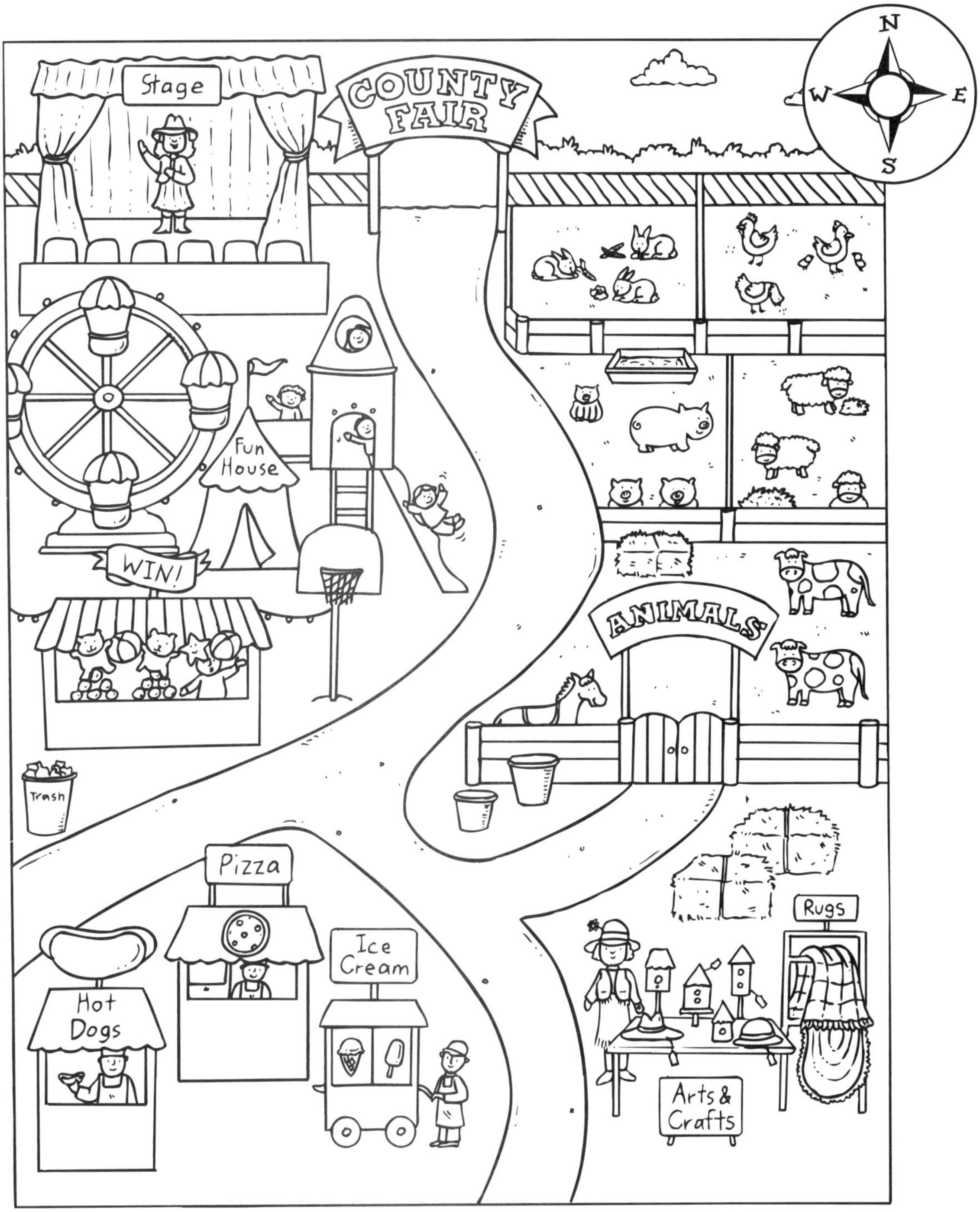

I like the ______________________________ at the county fair.

Name ______________________

Daily Geography

WEEK 28

A County Fair Map

Monday

1. The map shows a ________.

farm　　　county fair

2. The county fair is ________.

inside　　　outside

Tuesday

1. There are ________ animals at the fair.

farm　　　wild

2. There are ________ kinds of animals.

4　　　6

Wednesday

1. Which ride is at the county fair?

Ferris wheel　　　roller coaster

2. Name one kind of food sold at the fair.

____

Name ______________________________

Daily Geography

WEEK 28

A County Fair Map

Thursday

1. There are ________ in the arts and crafts area.

   games rugs

2. You can win a ________ at the fair.

   baseball hat teddy bear

Friday

1. A lady is ________ on the stage.

   eating singing

2. You enter the county fair at the ________ gate.

   north south

Challenge

1. Color your favorite area at the county fair.
2. Name your favorite area on the map.

WEEK 29

Daily Geography

ANSWER KEY

Monday
1. supermarket
2. food

Tuesday
1. canned foods
2. cereals

Wednesday
1. dairy products
2. bakery

Thursday
1. weighs
2. cake

Friday
1. candy
2. check-out

Challenge
Answers will vary, but students should color one product in each of the seven areas.

A Supermarket Map

Introducing the Map

Ask students to close their eyes and think about a supermarket in their minds. Can they picture where the bakery is located in the store? Where is the check-out stand? Is there candy or gum nearby? Where is the cereal aisle? Where are the milk and butter?

Tell students to open their eyes. What they just did was make a map of the supermarket. Share with students that when people set up a supermarket, they make a map of where they are going to put each area. The supermarket is organized by the kinds of products that go together. For example, all the cold products like milk and eggs have to be in refrigerated cases. A lot of supermarkets like to have the bakery near the door or the check-out stand. When people smell the breads and cookies, they get hungry and remember to buy those things. Tell students they might get confused if the cereal were in the aisle with the cleaning supplies. That wouldn't make much sense.

Show students the map of the supermarket. Name the different areas of the supermarket for students. Talk about the products that are in each area or aisle. Have students name a few products in the dairy case. Students should say things like milk, eggs, and butter. Talk about the scale next to the fruits and vegetables. Discuss how this is used to weigh them.

Talk about how people make a list of the things they will need. When they enter the store, they think about a route or a path to follow through the store. They choose the items they need from each aisle. When they are finished shopping, people go to the check-out. They buy the products with money.

In this lesson, students are introduced to a map of a supermarket. This lesson helps students realize that people plan carefully how to make stores more organized and attractive so people will buy the products in the store. You may choose to extend the lesson by introducing the terms grocer, grocery, and groceries.

Introducing Vocabulary

aisle
An aisle is a walkway between two rows.

check-out
The check-out is the place where you pay for things.

product
A product is something that is made and sold.
Cereal and milk are products.

supermarket
A supermarket is a large store that sells food.

Name

A Supermarket Map

The supermarket is where you buy products. Products are things that are made and sold.

Name ____

Daily Geography

WEEK 29

A Supermarket Map

Monday

1. The map shows a ________.

   shoe store supermarket

2. You can buy ________ at this supermarket.

   shoes food

Tuesday

1. What is in aisle 1?

   canned foods cereals

2. What is in aisle 2?

   canned foods cereals

Wednesday

1. What is in aisle 3?

   dairy products fruits and vegetables

2. What is next to the meat counter?

   bakery check-out

Name ____________________

Daily Geography

A Supermarket Map

WEEK 29

Thursday

1. The scale ________ the fruits and vegetables.

   counts   weighs

2. Which one is not in the dairy case?

   cake   butter   milk

Friday

1. Which one is a product in this supermarket?

   candy   check-out

2. Where do you pay for your food?

   bakery   check-out

Challenge

Color one product from each area of the supermarket.

WEEK 30

Daily Geography

Homes in a Community

Introducing the Map

Ask students to name different kinds of homes people live in. They will probably name such places as houses or apartments. Talk about how every community is made up of different types of homes. Tell students that many communities have one- and two-story houses, duplexes, apartments, and mobile homes. Define these different kinds of homes for students.

Show students the map of the fictitious community. Share with students that this community is a good example of a place that has different kinds of homes. The kinds of homes are divided into neighborhoods. Each of the neighborhoods has a name. Read the names of the neighborhoods for the students. Further explain *Duplex Row.* Tell students that a duplex is two houses joined by a wall. Building duplexes helps to save room in a community. There are six homes in this neighborhood.

Talk about the streets that the homes are on. Help students to see that the one-story houses and the duplexes are on Baker Street. The two-story houses and the mobile homes are on Roll Street. The apartments are on Candy Lane. Also, help them to see that no houses open onto Cookie Street. Discuss how each home would have its own address on those streets.

Ask students to think about which kind of home they would like to live in. They will be adding a home to the empty area on the map for the challenge question.

In this lesson, students are introduced to different kinds of housing in a community. Share with students that whatever kind of house they have, it is a home where they live and where they belong. They are an important part of the community.

Introducing Vocabulary

apartment

An apartment is a set of rooms to live in. Apartments are in a big building.

community

A community is a group of people who live together in the same area.

duplex

A duplex is two houses joined by a wall.

house

A house is a building where people live.

mobile home

A mobile home is a large trailer that people live in.

neighborhood

A neighborhood is a small area in a city where people live.

street

A street is a road in a town or city. Most streets have buildings on both sides.

ANSWER KEY

Monday
1. homes
2. streets

Tuesday
1. 3
2. 4

Wednesday
1. duplex
2. apartments

Thursday
1. 6
2. Sweet

Friday
1. Baker Street
2. empty lot

Challenge
Students should draw their favorite kind of home in the empty lot on the map.

Name

Homes in a Community

Name ____________________________________

Daily Geography

Homes in a Community

WEEK 30

Monday

1. The map shows ________ in a community.

   homes   parks

2. All the homes are on ________.

   highways   streets

Tuesday

1. Sweet Homes has ________ homes.

   3   6

2. Honey Mobile Homes has ________ homes.

   2   4

Wednesday

1. A ________ is two houses joined by a wall.

   duplex   mobile home

2. Candy Lane has ________.

   apartments   duplexes

Name ______________________________

Daily Geography

WEEK 30

Homes in a Community

Thursday

1. How many homes are on Duplex Row?

   4 6 8

2. ________ Homes is on Roll Street.

   Sugar Sweet

Friday

1. Which street runs north and south?

   Baker Street Cookie Street

2. What is east of Sugar Homes?

   park empty lot

Challenge

Draw your favorite kind of home on the map.

WEEK 31

Daily Geography

ANSWER KEY

Monday
1. community helpers
2. fire

Tuesday
1. hospital
2. school

Wednesday
1. library
2. post office

Thursday
1. bus
2. fire truck

Friday
1. together
2. ambulance

Challenge
Students should circle one community helper and color the place where that helper would work on the map.

Community Helpers

Introducing the Map

Ask students to name some community helpers in their area. They might name people like police officers, firefighters, and teachers. Explain to students that communities have people and places that help to take care of the needs of a community. They work together to help the community. Some services in a community include such places as a police station, fire station, hospital, post office, school, and library.

Show students the map of the fictitious community. Please note that only community services are shown on this map. Read and discuss the different services on this map. Talk about how the hospital, police station, and fire station help with emergencies in a community. Talk about the kinds of emergencies a community might have. Discuss how police officers and firefighters help to keep people safe. Talk about how many people in the schools and libraries help children and adults learn. The post office is a helpful place, too. That is where important letters and packages are mailed. Be sure to talk about the vehicles that provide services such as fire trucks, police cars, ambulances, and school buses.

In this lesson, students are introduced to some important places in a community. The people who work in these places serve to help the people in the community. You may wish to extend the lesson by helping the students understand that everybody in the community helps to pay for these kinds of services. You may also choose to have students learn the term *community services.*

Introducing Vocabulary

community
A community is a group of people who live together in the same area.

community services (not included in the glossary)
Community services are places that help people in a community. Police stations and schools are community services.

emergency
An emergency is something serious that needs quick action. A fire is an emergency.

Name

Community Helpers

A community has people who help you. The community helpers work together. They keep you safe and healthy. They help you learn and grow.

Name ______________________________

Daily Geography

Community Helpers

WEEK 31

Monday

1. The map shows the buildings where ________ work.

   community helpers   apartments

2. The map shows a ________ station.

   fire   gas

Tuesday

1. Where do you go if you are sick?

   hospital   post office

2. Where do you go to learn?

   hospital   school

Wednesday

1. Where can you check out books?

   library   post office

2. Where do you mail a letter?

   library   post office

Name ______________________________

Daily Geography

Community Helpers

WEEK 31

Thursday

1. A ________ takes children to school.

   bus truck

2. A ________ uses a siren.

   fire truck school bus

Friday

1. Community helpers work ________.

   alone together

2. What is used for an emergency?

   dump truck ambulance

Challenge

Which community helper would you like to be?

bus driver	firefighter	mail carrier	police officer
doctor	librarian	nurse	teacher

1. Circle one community helper.
2. Color the place where you would work on the map.

WEEK 32

Daily Geography

ANSWER KEY

Monday

1. Iowa
2. farms

Tuesday

1. 
2. 

Wednesday

1. corn
2. soybeans

Thursday

1. hogs
2. animals

Friday

1. beef cattle
2. milk

Challenge

Answers will vary. Students should color one animal and one plant on the map.

Farms in Iowa

Introducing the Map

Explain to students that people depend on the land for many needs. People change the land to build houses, grow plants, and to raise animals. Tell students that in many parts of the United States people use the land for farming.

Show students the map of Iowa. Tell students that Iowa is a top farm state. Read how many farms there are in Iowa. Tell students that Iowa is in an area of the United States where the land is made up of large plains that provide rich soil. The rich soil is good for planting. Have students look at the map key to see that Iowa grows corn and soybeans. Tell students that Iowa has four seasons. In the spring, plants like corn and soybeans are planted in fields. During the spring and summer, Iowa gets rain and plenty of sunshine. This makes the plants sprout and grow. Iowa farmers have an old saying about how corn grows: "Knee high by the 4th of July." This means that if the corn is at least knee high by the 4th of July, the corn will be ready for picking in the fall. After the plants are picked in the fall, the land rests for the winter. Share with students that Iowa ranks first in the nation for producing corn and soybeans. Tell students that one farm family in Iowa can grow enough food to feed 279 people.

Talk about the animals that are raised in Iowa. Have students look at the map key to see that Iowa raises beef cattle, dairy cows, and hogs (fully grown pigs). You may want to tell students that these animals are called livestock. Livestock are animals that are raised to sell. Iowa ranks first in the country for pork (hogs). Farmers also raise beef cattle and dairy cows. You may wish to share with students that Iowa ranks 8th in beef (cattle) and 12th for milk (dairy cows).

In this lesson, students should begin to understand that land has many uses. One important use is for farming.

Introducing Vocabulary

farm

A farm is an area of land.
It is used to grow plants and raise animals.

Name

Farms in Iowa

There are 87,000 farms in Iowa. Iowa grows the most corn. Iowa grows the most soybeans. Iowa raises the most hogs. Iowa is an important farm state.

Map Key	
Animals Raised	**Plants Grown**
 Beef Cattle	 Corn
 Dairy Cows	 Soybeans
 Hogs	

Name ____________________

Daily Geography

WEEK 32

Farms in Iowa

Monday

1. The map shows the state of ________.

   Iowa Texas

2. There are 87,000 ________ in Iowa.

   farms ranches

Tuesday

1. Which symbol stands for dairy cows?

2. Which symbol stands for soybeans?

Wednesday

1. Iowa grows the most ________.

   corn hay

2. Corn and ________ are plants.

   hogs soybeans

Name ______________________________

Daily Geography

WEEK 32

Farms in Iowa

Thursday

1. Iowa raises the most ________.

   ducks   hogs

2. Dairy cows and hogs are ________.

   animals   plants

Friday

1. Iowa is number 8 in the United States for ________.

   dairy cows   beef cattle

2. Dairy cows give us ________.

   eggs   milk

Challenge

1. Pretend you are a farmer.
2. Choose one animal to raise.
3. Color the animal on the map.
4. Choose one plant to grow.
5. Color the plant on the map.

WEEK 33

Visit California!

Introducing the Map

Ask students to name a state they would like to visit and tell why. An example might be the state of Hawaii from Week 17. Hawaii is made up of islands. They could swim or surf in the Pacific Ocean. They could see the volcanoes erupting on the big island.

Show students the map of California. Have students look at the small map of the United States to see where California is located. Explain to students that millions of people like to go to California on vacation. Talk about how California has land and water that provide fun for visitors. California is on the Pacific Ocean where people swim, fish, boat, and watch whales. Lake Tahoe is a favorite vacation spot. The Mojave Desert has the hottest spot in the United States. It is called Death Valley.

There are beautiful national parks to visit. Three are shown on this map. Share with students that national parks are places set aside to enjoy nature. The Redwood National Park has the tallest trees in the United States. Yosemite National Park has waterfalls to see, high cliffs to climb, and forests to walk through. There is an active volcano at Lassen Volcanic National Park.

The cities along the coast of California provide many things to do. San Francisco has the famous Golden Gate Bridge. Monterey has one of the world's best aquariums. It has 550 different kinds of fish and other ocean animals. It is famous for its sea otters, jellyfish, sharks, and sea turtles, just to name a few.

Los Angeles is the second-largest city in the United States. Hollywood, where many movies and television shows are made, is in Los Angeles. Anaheim is famous for Disneyland. The San Diego Zoo has more than 12,000 animals.

In this lesson, students learn how a map can help them plan which places they want to visit in California. Tell students that every state in the United States has many fun places to visit. Share with students that when people want to visit a state, they get maps to help them plan where to go. Now that students have looked at this tourist map of California, ask them which place they would like to visit the most.

Introducing Vocabulary

tourist

A tourist is a person who travels on vacation.

tourist map

A tourist map shows interesting places to visit.

ANSWER KEY

Monday

1. California
2. tourist map

Tuesday

1. travels
2. Pacific

Wednesday

1. Disneyland
2. Los Angeles

Thursday

1. San Diego Zoo
2. Mojave Desert

Friday

1. Redwood
2. Channel Islands

Challenge

1. Answers will vary. Students should choose one place in California and color it.
2. Answers will vary. Students should name one place to visit.

Name

Visit California!

This is a tourist map of California. It shows fun places to visit.

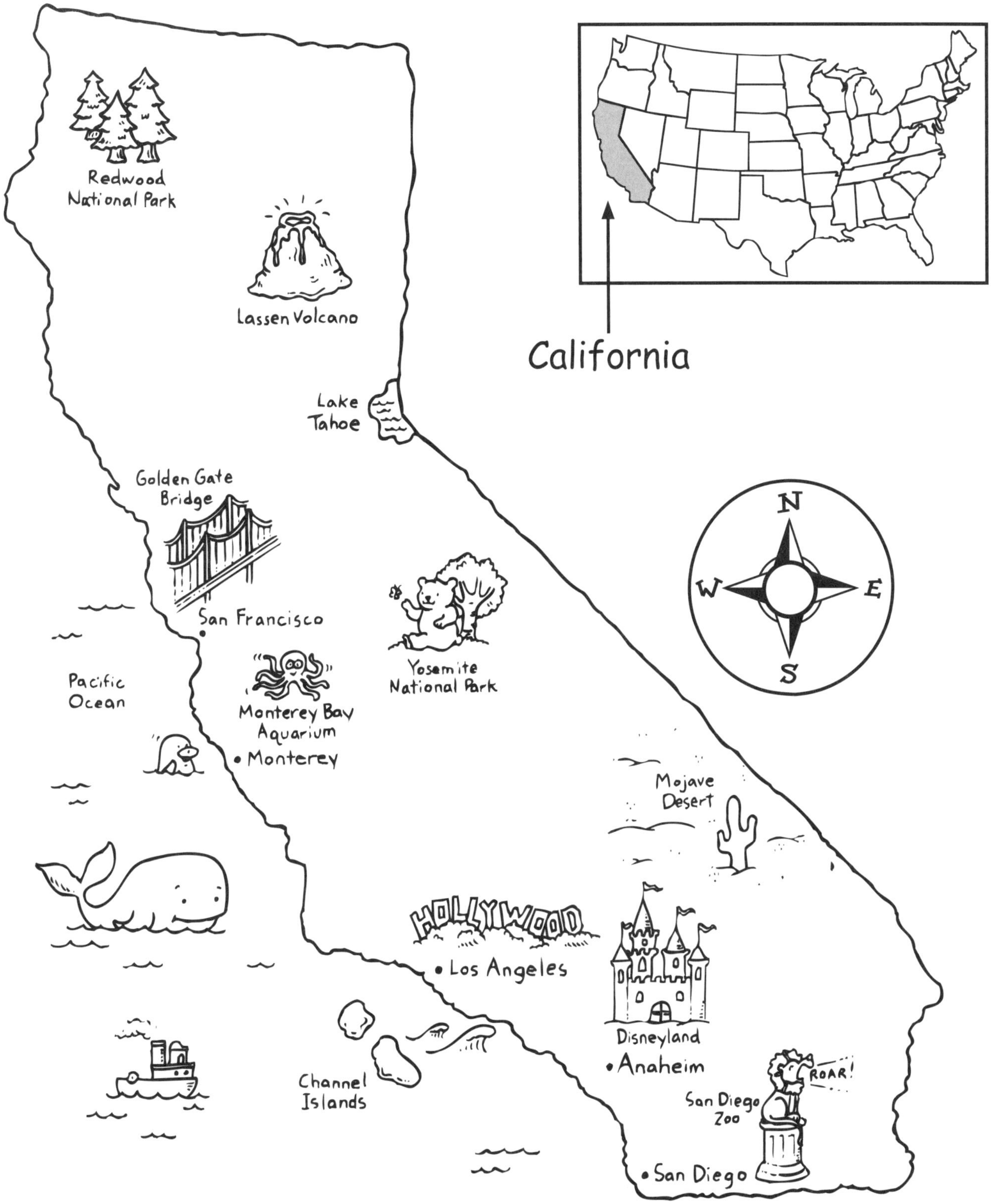

I would like to visit ______________________________.

Name ________________________________

Daily Geography

WEEK 33

Visit California!

Monday

1. The map shows the state of ________.

   California   Texas

2. What kind of map is shown?

   tourist map   weather map

Tuesday

1. A tourist is a person who ________.

   farms   travels

2. California borders the ________ Ocean.

   Atlantic   Pacific

Wednesday

1. What can you see in Anaheim?

   Disneyland   Mojave Desert

2. Which city is Hollywood in?

   Los Angeles   San Francisco

Name ______________________________

Daily Geography

Visit California!

WEEK 33

Thursday

1. Where can you see lions?

   Monterey Bay Aquarium   San Diego Zoo

2. ________ is a very hot place in California.

   Lake Tahoe   Mojave Desert

Friday

1. ________ National Park is in the north part of the state.

   Redwood   Yosemite

2. What islands can you visit in California?

   ____

Challenge

Be a tourist in California!

1. Choose your favorite place to visit. Color it on the map.
2. Name your favorite place on the map.

WEEK 34

Daily Geography

ANSWER KEY

Monday
1. Alaska
2. Juneau

Tuesday
1. 
2. 4

Wednesday
1. 
2. 

Thursday
1. trees
2. Barrow

Friday
1. oil
2. in water and on land

Challenge
Students should color the oil black, the gold yellow, the lumber brown, the crab red, the fish pink, and the oceans blue.

Skill: Natural Resources — Essential Element 5: Standard 16

Natural Resources of Alaska

Introducing the Map

Tell students that things found in nature are important to people. Materials found in nature are called natural resources. Examples of natural resources are things like water, forests, soil, animals, and minerals.

Show students the map of Alaska. Look at the small map of North America to see where Alaska is located. Talk about how Alaska is not connected to the rest of the United States. Alaska is the largest state in the United States. It is the 49th state. The United States was happy when Alaska became a state. Alaska has many natural resources that the United States needs.

Look at the map key to name the natural resources of Alaska. Talk about how Alaska has oil. Oil comes from under the ground. It is drilled and pumped into pipelines. Have students look at the map key to find an oil well and then locate it on the map. Oil is found in both northern and southern Alaska. Oil is important to people. Some people call oil "black gold" because it is so valuable. It is used as a fuel. Gasoline, which is used in cars, trucks, and other vehicles, is made from oil. Oil is used to heat some homes and businesses. Oil is used to make pavement for roads, streets, and sidewalks. Anything plastic has oil in it.

Next, tell students that gold is a mineral. Over 100 years ago, gold was discovered in Alaska. Many people went to Alaska to get rich. Today, gold is still mined in Alaska. Gold is used as money and is found in jewelry. Find the gold bar on the map key. Then have students count the number of places that have gold.

Tell students that Alaska has many forests. Trees in the forest are natural resources. Alaska has many national forests that are protected. Cutting trees for lumber is a big industry in Alaska. Only a certain amount is taken each year. Locate the lumber mills in Alaska.

Fishing is another big industry in Alaska. Alaska has many rivers. Alaska is famous for its salmon. Halibut is another kind of fish that is common. Fishermen from all over the world come to Alaska to fish for salmon and halibut. Alaska is also famous for its king crabs.

In this lesson, students are introduced to the term *natural resources.* They find out that Alaska is rich in natural resources. Only a few resources of Alaska have been highlighted for this lesson.

Introducing Vocabulary

natural resources

Natural resources are things found in nature.
They are useful to people.
Oil, gold, and fish are natural resources.

Name

Natural Resources of Alaska

Alaska has natural resources. Natural resources are things found in nature. Natural resources are all useful to people.

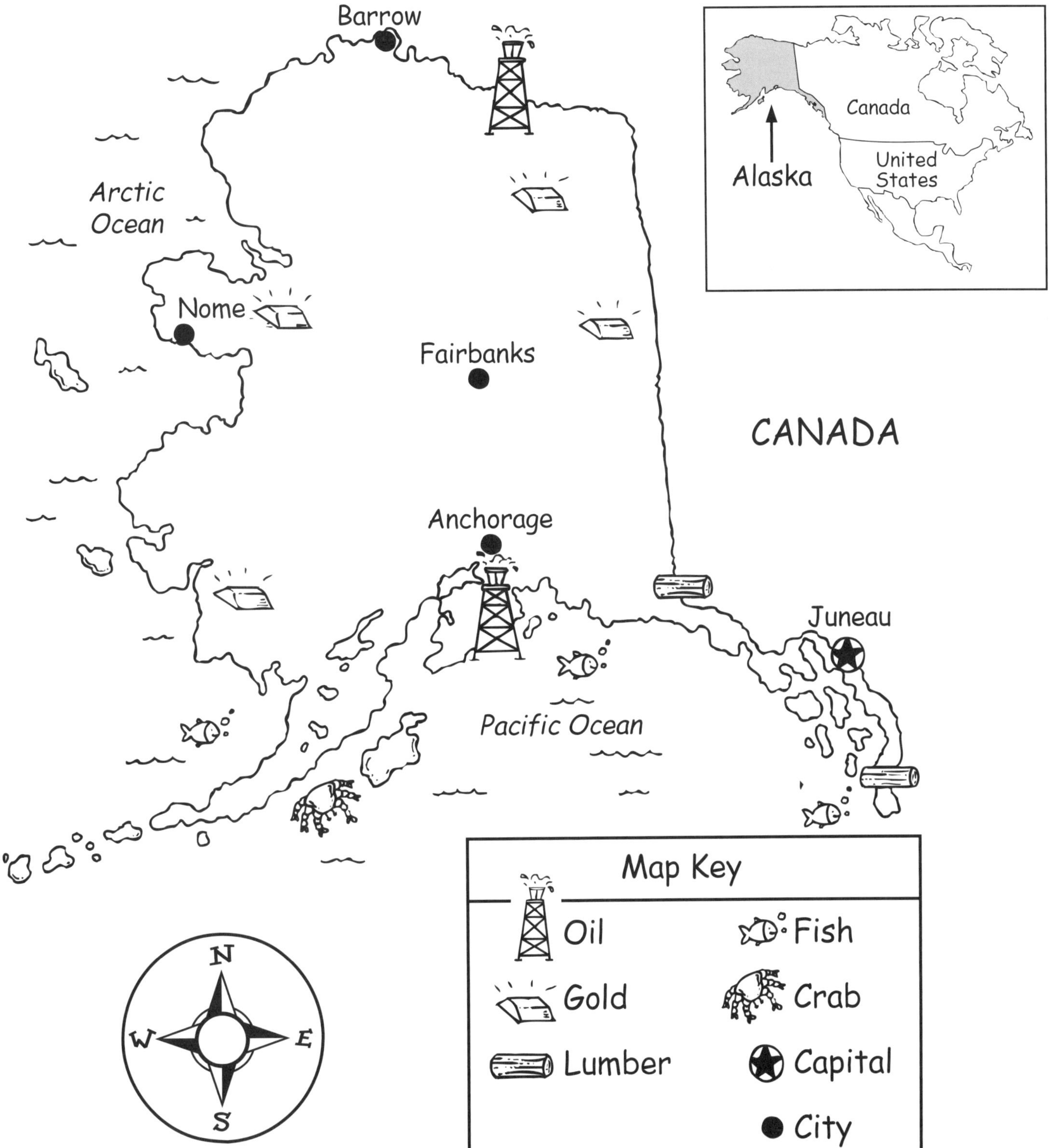

Name ____________________

Daily Geography

WEEK 34

Natural Resources of Alaska

Monday

1. The map shows the state of ________.

   Alaska California

2. Which city is the capital of Alaska?

   Anchorage Juneau

Tuesday

1. Which symbol stands for gold?  

2. There are ________ areas where gold is found.

   2 4

Wednesday

1. Which symbol stands for lumber?  

2. What is found in the Pacific Ocean?  

Name ______________________________

Daily Geography

WEEK 34

Natural Resources of Alaska

Thursday

1. Lumber comes from ________.

   trees　　　　fish

2. Which city is in the north?

   Barrow　　　　Fairbanks

Friday

1. Which natural resource is near Anchorage?

   oil　　　　gold

2. Natural resources are found ________.

   only in water　　　　only on land　　　　in water and on land

Challenge

1. Color the oil black.
2. Color the gold yellow.
3. Color the lumber brown.
4. Color the crab red.
5. Color the fish pink.
6. Color the oceans blue.

A Frontier Town

Introducing the Map

Tell students that long ago when the United States was young, most people lived on farms. Then people started to settle in small towns on the frontier. The frontier was the part of our country that was not settled yet. People moved to areas out west where they could get more land. Ask students to think about what life must have been like back then.

Show students the map of the frontier town. Tell students this is what a town looked like in the 1860s, or about 150 years ago. This town could have been in California. Talk about this old-fashioned town and what kinds of stores and buildings were in it. Compare and contrast the old with the new. For example, the general store was a place where people came to buy food, clothing, and all kinds of supplies. Ask students where people buy food and clothing today. Today we have supermarkets and clothing stores. Talk about the town sheriff. He was the man who made sure people obeyed the law. Today we have police officers and sheriffs who help people obey the law.

Tell students about the pony express. The pony express riders brought people their mail all the way from Missouri to California. That is about 2,000 miles. New riders took over every 100 miles. Today the mail comes very fast through post offices across the country and around the world.

Point out the one hotel and one bank in town. The barn was used for horses, and the blacksmith worked there. He put new horseshoes on the horses. Stagecoaches and wagons were pulled by horses. Now people use cars, buses, trains, and airplanes for transportation.

In this lesson, students begin to understand that frontier towns sprang up all over the West. Some frontier towns grew into larger towns. Some grew into large cities like Los Angeles, California. Students will begin to understand what the past was like by looking at maps from long ago. Students are also able to compare the workings of a frontier town with the place where they live.

Introducing Vocabulary

frontier town

A frontier town is a town from long ago.

WEEK 35

Daily Geography

ANSWER KEY

Monday
1. frontier town
2. long ago

Tuesday
1. hotel
2. General Store

Wednesday
1. barn
2. mail

Thursday
1. horses
2. blacksmith

Friday
1. years
2. bank and hotel

Challenge

Answers will vary. Students should write what they would like to do in the frontier town. One example might be to ride a horse.

Name

A Frontier Town

This map shows a town from long ago.
What was life like 150 years ago?

Name ______________________________

Daily Geography

WEEK 35

A Frontier Town

Monday

1. The map shows a ________.

   frontier town   city

2. The map shows how a town looked ________.

   long ago   today

Tuesday

1. The map shows a ________.

   hotel   hospital

2. Where did people go to buy things?

   General Store   Pony Express

Wednesday

1. The blacksmith worked in a ________.

   barn   hotel

2. The pony express delivered ________.

   food   mail

Name ______________________________

Daily Geography

WEEK 35

A Frontier Town

Thursday

1. People traveled on ________.

    airplanes   horses

2. Who makes horseshoes?

    blacksmith   sheriff

Friday

1. The map shows a town 150 ________ ago.

    days   years

2. Which buildings have the same names that we use today?

    bank and hotel   blacksmith and general store

Challenge

Pretend you live in this frontier town. What would you like to do? Write your answer on the map.

WEEK 36

Daily Geography

A Neighborhood Plan

Introducing the Map

Ask students to name places in their neighborhood. They might name such places as a park, school, video store, or a fire station. Discuss how hard it would be to plan a new neighborhood. Ask what they would like to see in a new neighborhood.

Show students the map of a fictitious neighborhood. Read the caption at the top of the page. Talk about the different parts of the neighborhood. Read the labels and identify the different streets. Help students understand that a street can also be called an avenue or a lane. Students will notice that this neighborhood has houses, a school, a Quick Stop (gas and food), and a bus stop.

Students should also notice the empty lot. Talk about how some neighborhoods have areas that are not very nice looking. That is sometimes true of empty lots. People in neighborhoods want the area to look nice. They want their neighborhood to be safe. As a class, make a list of things that could be built on the empty lot to help the neighborhood. Examples might include a library, a park, a police station, a swimming pool, or a shopping center. Students will be asked to draw something in the empty lot on the challenge question.

In this lesson, students begin to understand that communities have to plan for the needs of each neighborhood. They have to plan for the future.

Introducing Vocabulary

empty lot

An empty lot is a piece of land that has not been used.

neighborhood

A neighborhood is a small area in a city where people live.

street

A street is a road in a town or city.
Most streets have buildings on both sides.

ANSWER KEY

Monday

1. neighborhood
2. 4

Tuesday

1. Rose Avenue
2. school

Wednesday

1. Quick Stop
2. bus stop

Thursday

1. Center Street
2. houses

Friday

1. a neighborhood
2. an empty lot

Challenge

Answers will vary. Examples of drawings might be a library, a park, a swimming pool, or a shopping center.

Name

A Neighborhood Plan

The map shows a neighborhood. There is an empty lot.

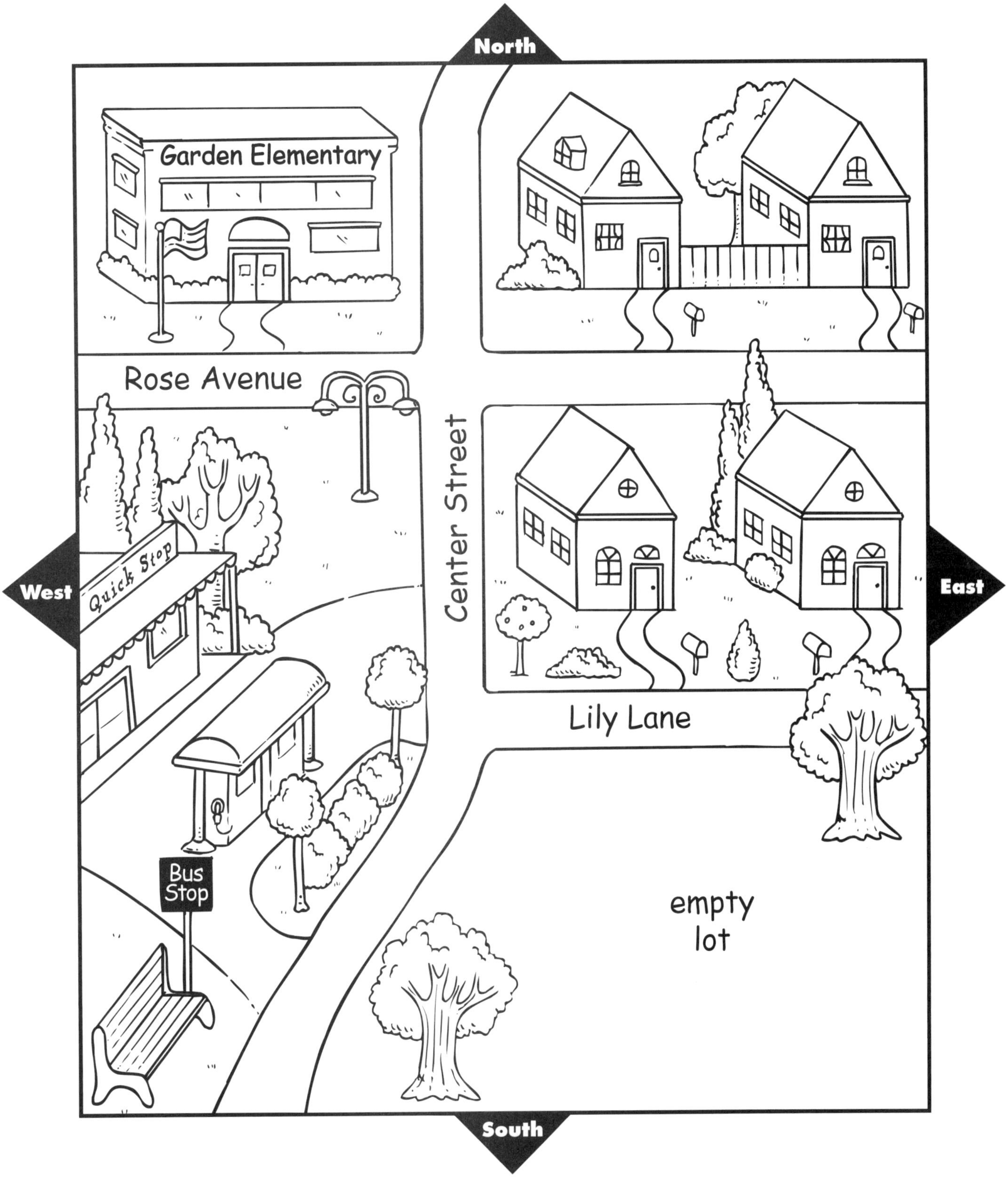

Name ____________________

Daily Geography

WEEK 36

A Neighborhood Plan

Monday

1. The map shows a ________.

   big city neighborhood

2. There are ________ houses in the neighborhood.

   4 6

Tuesday

1. The houses are on Lily Lane and ________.

   Center Street Rose Avenue

2. Garden Elementary is a ________.

   bus stop school

Wednesday

1. Where can people go to get gas?

   Garden Elementary Quick Stop

2. What is south of the Quick Stop?

   bus stop flag

Name ______________________________

Daily Geography

A Neighborhood Plan

WEEK 36

Thursday

1. Which street runs north and south?

   Center Street   Rose Avenue

2. What is north of Lily Lane?

   empty lot   houses

Friday

1. Which one is the smallest area?

   a city   a neighborhood   a state

2. What is a piece of land called that has not been used?

   a farm   an empty lot

Challenge

What would you build on the empty lot? Make a plan.
Draw it on the map.

Geography Glossary

belongs to:

____

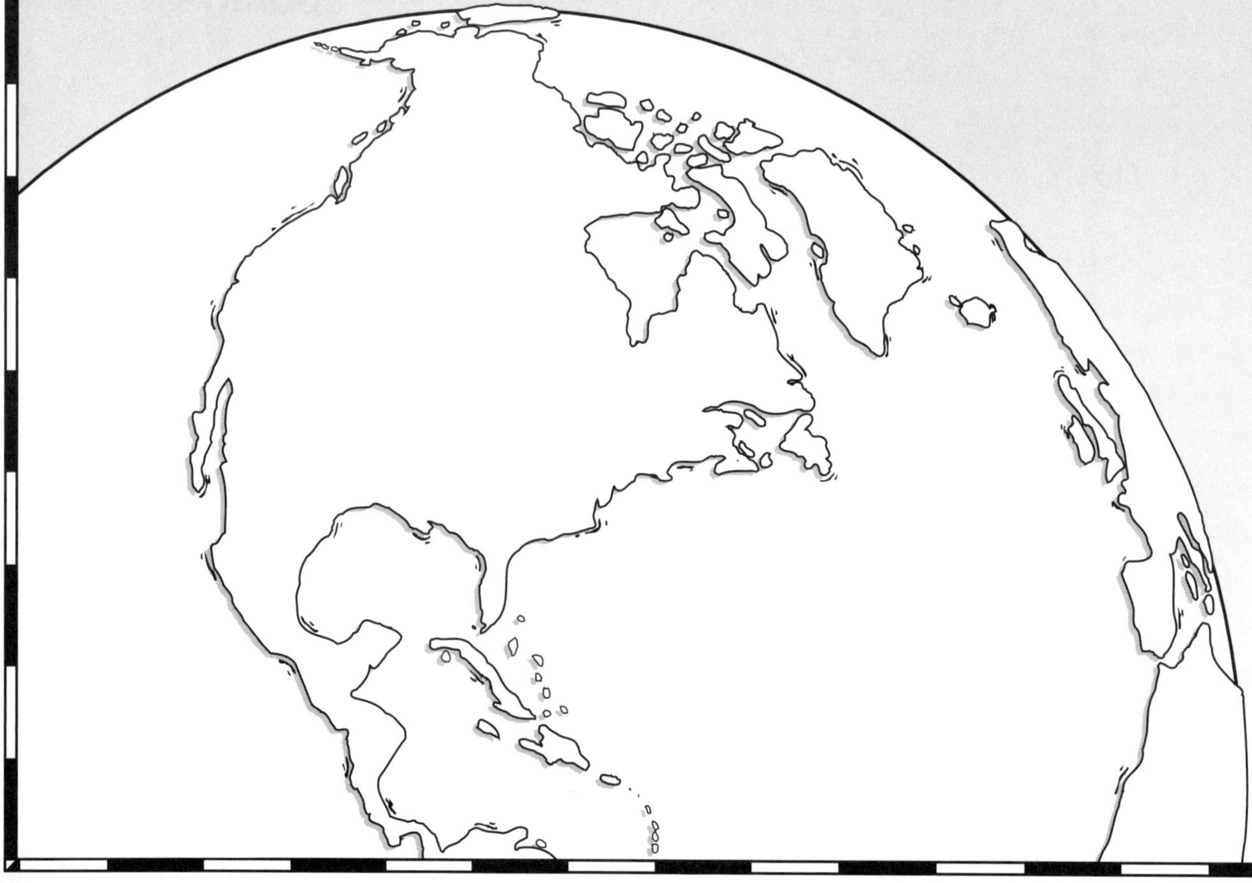

adobe

Adobe is a brick made of clay.
It is mixed with straw and dried in the sun.

aisle

An aisle is a walkway between two rows.
People walk down aisles in a supermarket.

apartment

An apartment is a set of rooms to live in.
Apartments are in a big building.

border

A border is a line between two places.
Maps show borders between states or countries.

camp

A camp is an outdoor place with tents.

canyon

A canyon is a deep valley with steep sides.

capital

A capital is a special city.
It is where the leaders of the state work.

carnival

A carnival is a fair with rides and games.

check-out

A check-out is the place where you pay for things.

city

A city is a very large or important town.

community

A community is a group of people who live together in the same area.

compass rose

A compass rose is a symbol on a map. It shows directions such as north, south, east, and west.

continent

A continent is a large area of land. North America is a continent.

country

A country is a land and the people who live there. The United States is a country.

countryside

Countryside is land away from cities and towns.

county fair

A county fair is an outdoor show.
A county fair shows animals and has fun things to do.

custom

A custom is a special way that people do things.
Going to a county fair every year is a custom.

desert

A desert is a dry, sandy, or rocky area of land.

direction

A direction tells where something is found.
The four main directions are north, south, east, and west.

downtown

Downtown is a city's main business area.

duplex

A duplex is two houses joined by a wall.

Earth

Earth is the planet where we live.

emergency

An emergency is something serious that needs quick action. A fire is an emergency.

empty lot

An empty lot is a piece of land that has not been used.

enter

To enter is to go into a place.

exit

The exit is the way out of a place.

farm

A farm is an area of land.
It is used to grow plants and raise animals.

floor

A floor is the story of a building.
A three-story building has 3 floors.

forest

A forest is a large area covered with many trees.

frontier town

A frontier town is a town from long ago.

globe

A globe is a model of Earth.

habitat

A habitat is a place where a plant or animal lives.
A habitat gives food, water, and shelter.
A desert is a habitat.

highway

A highway is a main road.

hill

A hill is land that rises above the land around it.
It is not as high as a mountain.

house

A house is a building where people live.

island

An island is land with water all around it.

lake

A lake is a body of water with land all around it.

landmark

A landmark is an important place or building.
A zoo is a landmark.

map

A map is a drawing of a place as seen from above.
A map shows where things are.

map key

A map key shows the symbols on a map.
It tells what each symbol stands for.

mobile home

A mobile home is a large trailer that people live in.

mountain

A mountain is land that rises very high above the land around it. It is higher than a hill.

natural resources

Natural resources are things found in nature.
They are useful to people.
Oil, gold, and fish are natural resources.

neighborhood

A neighborhood is a small area in a city where people live.

ocean

An ocean is a large body of water.
Earth has five oceans.

plain

A plain is flat land.

population

The population is the total number of people who live in a place.

product

A product is something that is made and sold. Cereal and milk are products.

river

A river is a large stream of water that flows across the land.

route

A route is a way to go from one place to another.

rural area

A rural area is where farms are. It is in the countryside.

rural route

A rural route is a farm road.

season

A season is one of the four parts of the year. The seasons are fall, winter, spring, and summer.

skyscraper

A skyscraper is a very tall building.

state

A state is part of a country.
There are 50 states in the United States.

street

A street is a road in a town or city.
Most streets have buildings on both sides.

supermarket

A supermarket is a large store that sells food.

symbol

A symbol is a drawing that stands for something real.

title

A title is the name of the map.
It tells what the map is about.

tourist

A tourist is a person who travels on vacation.

tourist map

A tourist map shows interesting places to visit.

town

A town is a place where people live and work.
A town is smaller than a city.

trail

A trail is a path you follow.

volcano

A volcano is a mountain that has an opening.
Lava, gases, and ashes spill out of the opening.

waterfall

A waterfall is a stream of water falling from a high place.

weather

Weather is what the air is like at a certain place and time.
Warm and sunny is a kind of weather.

woods

Woods is a small area with many trees.

world

The world is another name for Earth.

zoo

A zoo is a place where people come to see wild animals.

My Glossary Words

As you work through the weekly maps, you may find other words that are new to you. Write the definitions of those words on this page.